Thinking about Crime

THINKING
ABOUT
CRIME

JAMES Q. WILSON

Basic Books, Inc., Publishers

NEW YORK

Library of Congress Cataloging in Publication Data

Wilson, James Q
  Thinking about crime.

  Includes bibliographical references and index.
    1. Crime and criminals—United States—Addresses,
essays, lectures.   2. Criminal justice, Administration
of—United States—Addresses, essays, lectures.
I. Title.
HV6789.W53   364   74-25921
ISBN 0-465-08549-0

TO

Pete and Pat

Who Always Understood

Contents

Contents

Acknowledgments

TWO of the articles on which chapters of this book are based were written with the aid of coauthors. I should like to acknowledge their valuable assistance and to thank them for permitting me to reprint what in some cases was a joint project. They are Dr. Robert L. Dupont, M.D., with whom I wrote the original version of Chapter 1, and Dr. Mark H. Moore and Mr. I. David Wheat, Jr., with whom I wrote what now appears as Chapter 7.

I am grateful to the various publishers who have kindly permitted me to reprint, with alterations, material which first appeared under their auspices:

Chapter 1: "The Sick Sixties," *Atlantic Monthly*, 232 (October 1973): 91–98. Copyright © 1973, by the Atlantic Monthly Company, Boston, Mass. Reprinted with permission.

Chapter 2: "The Urban Unease: Community vs. City," *The Public Interest*, no. 12 (Summer 1968) pp. 25–39. Copyright 1968 by National Affairs, copyright 1974 by James Q. Wilson.

Chapter 3: "Crime and Criminologists," *Commentary*, 58 (July 1974): 47–53. Copyright © 1974 by the American Jewish Committee.

Chapter 4: "Crime and the Liberal Audience," *Commentary*, 51 (January 1971): 71–78. Copyright © 1971 by the American Jewish Committee.

Chapter 5: "Do the Police Prevent Crime?" *New York Times*

Sunday Magazine (October 6, 1974), p. 18. © 1974 by The New York Times Company. Reprinted by permission.

Chapter 6: Parts of "The Police in the Ghetto," in Robert F. Steadman, *The Police in the Community* (Baltimore: Johns Hopkins University Press, 1972), pp. 51–90, copyright 1972 by the Committee for Economic Development; and of "The Future Policeman," in "Future Roles of Criminal Justice Personnel" (prepared for Project Star of the American Justice Institute, March 1972).

Chapter 7: "The Problem of Heroin," *The Public Interest*, no. 29 (Fall 1972) pp. 3–28. Copyright 1972 by National Affairs, Inc., copyright 1974 by James Q. Wilson.

Chapter 8: "If Every Criminal Knew He Would Be Punished If Caught . . ." *New York Times Sunday Magazine* (January 28, 1973), p. 9 © 1973 by The New York Times Company. Reprinted by permission.

Chapter 9: "The Death Penalty," *New York Times Sunday Magazine* (October 28, 1973), p. 26. © 1973 by The New York Times Company. Reprinted by permission.

Introduction

THE essays that make up this book have a common theme. It is that the proper design of public policies requires a clear and sober understanding of the nature of man and, above all, of the extent to which that nature can be changed. Crime is not the only issue that evokes this theme, but it is one that does so dramatically and it happens to be one that I have, quite without intending it, found myself studying on and off for the last ten or twelve years.

These inquiries were prompted by no grand design but were begun episodically, often in response to a question put to me by a colleague, a government agency, or an editor. I say this not to apologize for unevenness in the chapters that follow (though there is much of that), but rather to call attention to the fact that, though the book was not written from beginning to end in one time period in accord with a single purpose, I have approached each of the topics with a more or less consistent perspective, often without realizing it.

That perspective is not easily stated, but I can begin by pointing out what it is not. It is not one that has been informed by much of what passes for public debate on the issue of crime. As I studied, first the police and then crime itself, I was struck with how remote from the reality I observed was the rhetoric I heard. Demands that the police "get tough" and "crack down" on crime seemed incongruous given what I knew, from hundreds of hours spent in patrol cars, about what the police actually spent their time doing. Public entertainments in which the climax of the mystery story was the arrest of the guilty party bewildered me because, in the real world, an arrest rarely ends anything. The arrested person is usually released within a few hours, will probably not come to trial for months, and, even if his guilt is determined, has an excellent chance of being returned to society promptly without any penalty at all. Most of those charged with offenses can be divided into two groups: those for whom arrest is an embarrassment and those for whom it is a mere inconvenience.

The intense debate over the evidentiary rules governing search and seizure, police interrogations, and the taking of confessions, while it illuminated some interesting legal and philosophic issues, had a hollow ring when recalled in the context of what actually happens in a police station house. Most persons arrested for the more common serious crimes, such as burglary and robbery, have been arrested under circumstances such that no confession is required, no searches need be conducted, and scarcely any police interrogation occurs. Often they are caught right in the act of robbing or burgling. Frequently there are witnesses to testify or stolen property that can be identified. Many—I should say most—of those arrested, far from wishing to remain silent behind their constitutionally protected rights, are eager to talk in order to see whether, by confessing to other crimes or implicating other persons, they can lighten the charges against them.

The claim that slum residents despise the police and refuse their aid, often made by nonslum residents who wish, for various reasons, to see the police in poor neighborhoods incapacitated or removed, is a strange claim if one has spent the night in a station house or patrol car. One observes the constant stream of humanity, much of it poor and black, seeking police assistance for every imaginable problem, from crime to marital disputes, broken windows to electric failures, drunkenness to terminal illness.

The passionate debate over the death penalty as a deterrent to murder is difficult to interpret when one remembers the murders one has actually seen. There is a night of drinking. The conversation turns to money or women. Rights are asserted and disputed, greed claimed and denied, sexual prerogatives demanded and rejected. A fight begins. Someone picks up a knife or a gun. A body falls, a neighbor screams, the police arrive, the culprit is encountered, still standing with the weapon in his hand, gazing in drunken bewilderment at his victim.

The theory that crime is an expression of the political rage of the dispossessed, rebelling under the iron heel of capitalist tyranny, leaves one wondering why virtually every nation in the world, capitalist, socialist, and communist, has experienced in recent years rapidly increasing crime rates. Such a theory also leaves one dissatisfied with the explanation it purports to offer for why fifteen-year-old boys tear a purse from the hands of a poor black woman on a subway train, why rioters loot each other's homes but not the bank on the corner, or why cars are stolen from parking lots and shipped, repainted, to big cities where they can be resold at bargain prices to affluent businessmen.

But above all, I found inexplicable the theories of human nature that seemed to be implicit in much of the public rhetoric about crime. "Men steal because they are poor and deprived." There is more crime in most poor neighborhoods than in most well-off ones, but even in poor communities most people do not steal. Furthermore, crime rose the fastest in this country at a time when the number of persons living in poverty or squalor was declining. No doubt many persons believe that crime produces higher incomes with less effort than available legitimate jobs. But those who are prepared to consider seriously the objective benefits of crime will surely give some, perhaps equal, attention to the objective costs of crime. Therefore, it cannot be simply the case that "men steal because they are poor." If objective conditions are used to explain crime, then the full statement must be: "Men steal because the benefits of stealing exceed the costs of stealing by a wider margin than the benefits of working exceed the costs of working." In short, spokesmen who use poverty as an explanation of crime should, by the force of their own logic, be prepared to consider the capacity of society to deter crime by raising the risks of crime. But they rarely do. Indeed, those who use poverty as an explanation are largely among the ranks of those who vehemently deny that crime can be deterred.

Advocates of increasing the harshness of penalties commit the same error, but in the opposite direction. "Man will not steal if the penalty is sufficiently severe." No doubt, very severe penalties will deter many people from stealing, *if* those who consider stealing believe the penalty is likely to be exacted; *if* the penalty, discounted by the chances of avoiding it, is of greater value than the proceeds of the crime, discounted by the chances of not getting away with it; and *if* there is another source of income (such as a job) that would produce greater net gains. The United States has, on the whole, the most severe set of criminal penalties in its lawbooks of any advanced Western nation; it also has the highest crime rate of most advanced Western nations. One reason may be that our penalties are so high that they are rarely imposed. Another may be that we have not only a high crime rate, but a high level of personal affluence and an abundant consumer economy. A person wishing to drive a fancy car may well conclude that the slight chance of having to pay a heavy penalty should he be caught stealing is more than outweighed by the immediate pleasure he will derive from having the car, a pleasure that he would have to defer for a long time, perhaps indefinitely, if he were content with the low-paying jobs available to him. Getting institutions to work as we want them to work (in this case, to impose *any* penalties, much less severe ones) and insuring that there exist attractive alternatives to the courses of action we do penalize are more important, and more difficult, tasks than changing a statute to read "twenty years in jail" instead of "ten years in jail."

"Crime and drug addiction can only be dealt with by attacking their root causes." I am sometimes inclined, when in a testy mood, to rejoin: "Stupidity can only be dealt with by attacking its root causes." I have yet to see a "root cause" or to encounter a government program that has successfully attacked it, at least with respect to those social problems that arise out of human volition rather than technological malfunction. But more importantly, the demand for causal solutions is, whether intended or not, a way of deferring any action and criticizing any policy. It is a cast of mind that inevitably detracts attention from those few things that governments can do reasonably well and draws attention toward those many things it cannot do at all.

Consider heroin addiction. For decades various public and private agencies tried to cure addicts, either by simply withdrawing them from heroin or, through the provision of various psychological and other services, by eliminating the "root causes" of their addiction. With few exceptions, these efforts failed. In the 1960s a massive law-enforcement effort was made to reduce the availability of heroin, and doctors began supplying addicts with methadone as an alternative. Methadone was not a "cure" for addiction, and of course neither was law enforcement. Indeed, methadone had some problems of its own. But methadone had one powerful advantage: As a relatively benign addictive drug that suppresses withdrawal pains, it is a powerful inducement for many addicts to enter and remain in treatment programs, and is a pharmacological tool for stabilizing the addict while in treatment and in the community. Whether the addict, thus stabilized, can improve himself and avoid relapsing into euphoria-seeking drug use depends on a number of things, not the least of which are his own motivation and the support given to him by employers and family. Meanwhile, law enforcement has made heroin much harder to find and, when found, both much less potent (i.e., more heavily diluted) and much more expensive. The combined effect of these two strategies, coupled (as government programs often must be if they are to work) with some fortuitous changes in slum life styles, has been to accomplish a dramatic reduction in several cities in the recruitment of new addicts and the death or imprisonment of many old ones.

Were the American public in a mood for celebrating their accomplishments rather than despairing over their failings, the modest, not unmixed, but substantial gains won in coping with heroin might be one such accomplishment. None of these gains were the result of attacking the "root causes" of addiction, however. Indeed, if policy had been made by those who insisted that only elimination of causes is a proper object for public action, methadone would never have been approved for wide clinical use, there would have been little or no law-enforcement effort, and there probably would have been an even greater growth in the size of the addict population.

It is difficult to state in positive terms what lessons I draw from such observations. I recall Reinhold Niebuhr's modest defense of democracy: Man is good enough to make it possible and bad enough to make it necessary. It might be restated thusly: Man is refractory enough to be unchangeable but reasonable enough to be adaptable. The institutions of governance created by man reflect his nature. Where an appropriate technology exists and the self-interest of persons can be linked to its operation, there are virtually no limits to what men in organizations can achieve. Where no such technology exists and the inducement is mere piety, there is scarcely anything an organization can do except grow and be meddlesome.

In thinking about popular responses to crime, I am struck by how keen and sure are people's awareness of their own problems and interests (thus, public opinion was well ahead of political opinion in calling attention to the rising problem of crime), how insightful is the public understanding of the causes of crime (the average person locates the principal cause right where criminologists, after much puzzling, have suggested it might be—in the attitudes formed by family and peer group), and how uncertain and dubious are many of the public's favorite remedies for crime (more police, tougher laws, better criminal rehabilitation). It is the duty of the statesman to try to take the confident instincts and immediate knowledge of the public and convert them, by persuasion and inducement, into reasonable policy proposals. American statesmen have not done that job very well when it comes to crime, nor have many of us who are supposed to advise them on how to do it given them very good advice.

This book, therefore, is as much about how to think about crime (which is to say, how to think about human nature in one of its less attractive forms) as it is about crime itself. I argue that a proper understanding of man and the publicly controllable forces to which he will respond, coupled with only moderate expectations about what can be accomplished under even the best of circumstances, is the essential place to begin any discussion of crime and its control.

The first part of this book describes our recent experience with crime and its impact on the community. The second part suggests how statesmen, criminologists, and politicians have thought about crime and how they might think better. The third part takes up some, but not all, of the ways of dealing with crime: better police, drug control, sentencing, corrections, and the death penalty. The final chapter offers some suggestions to improve our policies.

This last part does not purport to be a comprehensive review of crime strategies. I do not take up, for example, gun control. This is not because I believe that the ready availability of handguns has no effect on the incidence of assaults and murders (though it is exasperatingly hard to get good data, there is almost surely such a relationship), but rather because I am not sure what can be said at length about the problem. The subject has yet to be carefully investigated, and since I am dependent in much of this book on the research of others, I find myself with little to say. As to a proper way of coping with the problem, I am in general principle in favor of rather complete civilian disarmament but I am not yet certain how this can best be done.

Nor do I treat all of the problems of our criminal justice system. I have nothing to say about prosecutors and defense attorneys, but only out of ignorance, not from any insensitivity to their importance. I do not take up the problem of police and judicial corruption, though it exists and in some places is endemic. I am rather tolerant of some forms of civic corruption (if a good mayor can stay in office and govern effectively only by making a few deals with highway contractors and insurance agents, I do not get overly alarmed), but I am rather intolerant of those forms of corruption that debase the law-enforcement process, discredit its agents, or lead people to believe that equal justice is available only for a price. But beyond recording my anger at crooked cops and judges and urging police and judicial administrators to be tough and vigilant, I must confess to not knowing of any easy strategies that can be generally applied to solve the problem. I have spent a lot of time with honest police chiefs, and they do not know of any such strategies either.

Finally, I do not discuss what I regard as a major barrier to effective change in criminal justice—the tendency for decisions in this field to be unduly influenced by the organized interests of those whose behavior is to be changed. I refer to what might be called "criminal justice syndicalism": the rise in power of organized police and correctional officers and the continued power of tenured judges, powers which, though for many purposes quite desirable, have come to constitute a serious impediment to progress. The *reductio ad absurdum* of this process has been the emergence of prisoner unions which insist on participating in decisions as to whether any changes are to be made in the purposes and methods of prisons.

Throughout I use the word "crime" as if we all knew what this meant. Of course we do not. It is a term that covers everything from white-collar bank embezzlement to blue-collar rape, from offenses in which the victim is as much to blame as the perpetrator to those in which the victim is wholly innocent. Rather than burden the reader with countless distinctions and categories, I have instead adopted a simplifying rule: Unless otherwise stated or clearly implied, the word "crime" when used alone in this book refers to predatory crime for gain, the most common forms of which are robbery, burglary, larceny, and auto theft.

This book deals neither with "white-collar crimes" nor, except for heroin addiction, with so-called "victimless crimes." Partly this reflects the limits of my own knowledge, but it also reflects my conviction, which I believe is the conviction of most citizens, that predatory street crime is a far more serious matter than consumer fraud, antitrust violations, prostitution, or gambling, because predatory crime, for reasons set forth in Chapter 2, makes difficult or impossible the maintenance of meaningful human communities. Even those who agree with the greater importance of street crime may nonetheless argue that police preoccupation with "victimless crimes" seriously impedes their attention to more serious matters. I disagree. Though millions of persons are arrested each year for drunkenness, prostitution, and marijuana possession, and though one can raise grave questions about the propriety of arrest as a response to these behaviors, in fact, the police devote very few resources to these matters (for example, drunk arrests are as easy as traffic arrests and require only a few officers, or a little time from each officer, to produce large numbers). Furthermore, what is listed as a "drunk" arrest or a "marijuana" arrest is typically an arrest for another reason (disorderly conduct, a traffic violation) in which the presence of alcohol or marijuana leads to the imposition of more serious charges.

Most of the chapters that make up this book appeared earlier in the form of essays and articles. All have been revised for this book, some substantially. The revisions are not complete in that they do not take into account all the relevant research that has been done since the articles first appeared, but they do reflect such changes in my own thinking as has occurred since I first wrote them. I emphasize the revisions, perhaps in the vain hope that this will persuade the reader that what he holds in his hand is a book and not simply a collection of essays.

PART
I
CRIME

Chapter 1

Crime Amidst Plenty: The Paradox of the Sixties

IF in 1960 one had been asked what steps society might take to prevent a sharp increase in the crime rate, one might well have answered that crime could best be curtailed by reducing poverty, increasing educational attainment, eliminating dilapidated housing, encouraging community organization, and providing troubled or delinquent youth with counseling services. Such suggestions would have had not only a surface plausibility, but some evidence to support them. After all, crime was more common in slum neighborhoods than in middle-class suburbs, and the latter could be distinguished from the former by the income, schooling, housing, and communal bonds of their residents. To improve the material conditions of inner-city life would, of course, require a high level of national prosperity combined with programs aimed specifically at inner-city conditions. There was a confident conviction at the highest levels of the administrations of Presidents Kennedy and Johnson that this prosperity would be achieved and these programs devised.

They were right. Early in the decade of the 1960s, this country began the longest sustained period of prosperity since World War II, much of it fueled, as we later realized, by a semiwar economy. A great array of programs aimed at the young, the poor, and the deprived were mounted. Though these efforts were not made primarily out of a desire to reduce crime, they were wholly consistent with—indeed, in their aggregate money levels, wildly exceeded—the policy prescription that a thoughtful citizen worried about crime would have offered at the beginning of the decade.

Crime soared. It did not just increase a little; it rose at a faster rate and to higher levels than at any time since the 1930s and, in some categories, to higher levels than any experienced in this century. The mood of contentment and confidence in which the decade began was shattered, not only by crime, but by riots and war. American democracy, which seemingly had endured in part because, as David Potter phrased it, we were a "people of plenty" relieved of the necessity of bitter economic conflict, had in the 1960s brought greater plenty to more people than ever before in its history, and the result was anger, frustration, unrest, and confusion.

Various explanations were offered for the apparent failure of the American promise. Liberals first denied that crime *was* rising. Then, when the facts became undeniable, they blamed it on social programs that, through lack of funds and will, had not yet produced *enough* gains and on police departments that, out of prejudice or ignorance, were brutal and unresponsive. It was not made clear, of course, just why more affluence would reduce crime when some affluence had seemingly increased it, or why criminals would be more fearful of gentle cops than of

4

tough ones. Conservatives, exaggerating the crime increase, blamed it on a "soft" Supreme Court and a "permissive" attorney general on the apparent assumption—never defended, and in fact indefensible—that the Supreme Court and the attorney general could effectively manage the day-to-day behavior of the local police, and that the level of police effectiveness was directly related to the level of crime.

In fact, rising crime rates were not the only sign of social malaise during the 1960s. The prosperity of the decade was also accompanied by alarming rises in welfare rates, drug abuse, and youthful unemployment. During the 1960s we were becoming two societies—one affluent and worried, the other pathological and predatory. This development was first noticed by Andrew Brimmer and Daniel P. Moynihan, who separately but with equal dismay noted that, by the second half of the decade, blacks generally were improving their income positions but blacks in the inner slums were becoming worse off, that the educational attainments of the young generally had risen sharply but that many inner-city schools had virtually ceased to function, and that the work force was at an all-time high at the same time as were the welfare rolls.

It all began in about 1963. That was the year, to overdramatize a bit, that a decade began to fall apart.

Crime

IN 1946 there were in this country 6.9 murders per one hundred thousand population, the highest murder rate since 1937.[1] In the seventeen years that followed the end of World War II, the murder rate declined more or less steadily, so that by 1962 it was only 4.5 per one hundred thousand population—less than two-thirds of what it had been in 1946. In 1964 it showed a slight increase to 4.8, in 1965 another slight increase to 5.1, and in 1966 a larger increase to 5.6; by 1972 it stood at 9.4, higher than at any time since 1936.

Robbery is perhaps the most feared crime, inasmuch as it so often occurs among strangers, without warning, and involves the use or threat of force. It is not as accurately counted as murder, but, being serious and not involving friends, most of the serious cases are called to the attention of the police. In 1946 the robbery rate was 59.4 per one hundred thousand population, higher than it had been since 1935. Then robbery, like murder, began to show a long, slow decline in its incidence until, by 1959, the rate was only 51.2—a drop of 14 per cent. The following year it went up suddenly to 59.9, the largest one-year increase during any of the preceding seventeen years. For the next two years it held steady at about this same level, and then in 1963 it went up again; in 1964, again; and in 1965, again. By 1968 it had more than *doubled*, to 131.0.

Auto theft is also a more or less accurately counted crime: cars are insured, and victims must report the loss to collect their payments. This crime follows, until the 1960s, a pattern just opposite that for murder and robbery: the mid-1940s were a *low* point for auto theft, probably because the production of automobiles for civilian use had ended during World War II, so that by 1946 there were simply not many cars around that were worth stealing. The actual low point for auto theft came in 1949, when only 107.7 cars per one hundred thousand population were stolen. Then, as the country returned to a peacetime economy and new cars began rolling off the production lines, the auto theft rate began to drift upward. By 1960 it had risen to 181.6, an increase of almost 60 per cent. For a year or two the rate paused at this new high—new, at least, for any period since 1935. Then, from 1963 to 1964, it went up by the largest amount of any year since records were kept: over thirty points. In the language of the stock market chart makers, auto theft had "broken out," and from that year on it showed sharp annual increases. Put another way, from 1949 to 1961 auto theft increased each year on the average by fewer than seven cars stolen per one hundred thousand population. From 1962 to 1963 it increased at a rate of two and one-half times faster than in any preceding year, and from 1963 to 1964 at a rate over four times faster.

If the figures are to be believed, the increase in crime assumed epidemic proportions in the first few years of the 1960s. Interestingly, murder was somewhat slower to show this increase than robbery or auto theft. One reason for this difference may be the continued improvement in the delivery of emergency health care to people who have been assaulted: Speedy ambulance drivers and skilled doctors and nurses may have kept the homicide rate down by saving the lives of growing proportions of persons who have been shot or stabbed. (In 1933 there were six times as many crimes listed as aggravated assaults as there were those listed as homicides. By 1960 the ratio had increased to seventeen to one, a crude measure, perhaps, of the improvements resulting from radio-dispatched ambulances and new medical and surgical techniques.)

Drugs

DURING most of the 1950s, the number of narcotic-related deaths reported by the medical examiner in New York City hovered around one hundred a year.[2] In 1960 it touched two hundred for the first time since at least 1918, and perhaps ever. In 1961 there was a sudden, sharp increase to over three hundred, but the following year it dropped back again. In 1963 the number increased sharply again, and by 1967 had passed seven hundred a year and was still climbing. By the end of the decade, over twelve hundred New Yorkers who died each year either had taken a lethal overdose of a narcotic or had died of some other cause while being habitual narcotic users. Furthermore, the proportion of all narcotic-related deaths due to an overdose had increased: less than half of such deaths before 1961, but more than 80 per cent after 1971.

Before 1963, Atlanta probably had no more than about five hundred heroin users. By the end of the decade, the number of users had increased tenfold, to five thousand.

In Boston, the estimated number of heroin users never exceeded six hundred in the period between 1960 and 1963. Between 1963 and 1964, there was a sudden estimated increase of more than four hundred users. During the following year the increase was eight hundred. By the end of the decade, the number of Boston users, like the number of those in Atlanta, had increased tenfold.

Welfare

IN MARCH 1965, Daniel P. Moynihan, then an assistant secretary of labor, published a document entitled *The Negro Family*.[3] The study described the weakness of the family structure among a large minority of blacks and argued for a national policy to correct the causes of that weakness and to support processes that would strengthen such families. The conditions he described were not new: Since at least 1950 (the earliest figures included in the report), about one-fifth of black married women, as compared to about one twenty-fifth of white married women, were separated from their husbands. A large and growing number of these women with children but without husbands were on welfare (i.e., receiving Aid to Families of Dependent Children [AFDC]).

One fact appeared in the Moynihan report, however, that was utterly without precedent. Since 1948, the annual number of new AFDC cases paralleled almost precisely the unemployment rate for nonwhite males. Whenever the nonwhite unemploy-

8

ment rate went up, as it did in 1949, 1954, and 1957, the number of new welfare cases went up. All this was to be expected—indeed, it was exactly what most supporters of the AFDC plan desired. But in 1962–1963, a remarkable thing happened: The number of new persons admitted to AFDC started going up even though the unemployment rate was going *down*.

From 1961 to 1964, the unemployment rate for nonwhite males fell from 12.9 per cent to 9.1 per cent, but between 1962 and 1964 the number of new AFDC cases opened each year increased by almost sixty thousand. In short, entry onto the welfare rolls was for the first time being influenced by forces independent of general economic conditions, and of unemployment in particular. For decades the line plotting unemployment and the line plotting new AFDC cases were parallel; beginning in about 1960, they moved in opposite directions. From its graphic appearance, the phenomenon might be referred to as the "welfare scissors."

If a second edition of the study had been published in 1969, it would have shown that the scissors continued to open. By then, the nonwhite unemployment rate had fallen to 6.5 per cent, but the annual number of new AFDC cases had grown by 222 per cent.

The reasons for the increase in welfare applicants at a time when economic conditions were improving remains a matter of conjecture. Some saw the increase as the result of the rise in illegitimacy, especially among black children, but it is far from clear that this occurred (there have probably been important changes in the willingness to *report* a birth as illegitimate, but whether the actual *number* of such births has gone up is uncertain). If it occurred, the change took place in the first five years of 1960. From 1955 to 1960, the proportion of nonwhite births reported as illegitimate went from 20.2 per cent to 21.6 per cent, a trifling change; from 1960 to 1965, however, it rose from 21.6 to 26.3 per cent, an increase of better than one-fifth.

Nor is it clear that the rise in welfare consumption in the

early 1960s was the result of increasing proportions of women being deserted by their husbands. In 1960, 11 per cent of married nonwhite women were separated from their husbands; by 1966 it was still 11 per cent. (The proportion of divorced remained constant at 5 per cent.) The percentage of nonwhite female-headed households increased only slightly between 1960 and 1966.

What *is* clear is that a growing percentage of women eligible for AFDC began to apply for it, and to receive it. Welfare became either socially more attractive or administratively more accessible, or both. While only a minority of illegitimate children receive welfare, and while many women deserted by their husbands never apply for welfare, it now seems clear that in the early 1960s more and more of those eligible for such aid sought it and, in many cities, more and more of those seeking it got it.

Unemployment

THERE WERE only three years between 1947 and 1957 during which there were as many as one million young persons (ages sixteen to twenty-four) who were unemployed. Since 1958 there has been no year in which there were *fewer* than one million unemployed young adults, and by 1961 they numbered 1.5 million, almost twice as many as there had been in 1955. The rate of unemployment for young workers was on the order of 8 to 10 per cent between 1947 and 1957; from 1958 through 1964, it was never below 11 per cent.

The United States made enormous strides in providing jobs during the 1960s, but adults benefited more than young people. During a decade when the unemployment rate generally declined, the unemployment rate for persons sixteen to nineteen years of age actually increased, so that whereas the young made up only one-sixth of the unemployed in 1961, they accounted for more than one-quarter of it by 1971. In one year, 1963, the number of unemployed persons aged sixteen to nineteen increased by *one-fourth* to 17 per cent. As the Bureau of Labor Statistics was later to write, "In 1963, the relative position of teenagers began to deteriorate markedly." [4] Whereas before their unemployment was never more than two or three times greater than that of adults, after 1963 it was at least four times greater, and by 1968 was better than five times greater.

The increase in teenage and young adult unemployment was particularly sharp among nonwhites. Not only were a higher proportion of young nonwhites than young whites unemployed, but the increase in youth unemployment was greater for the former than for the latter: Between 1960 and 1963, which was the peak year for the decade, the unemployment rate among persons age sixteen to nineteen went up by 23 per cent for whites but by 28 per cent for nonwhites. In 1963 there were 176,000 unemployed young nonwhites, more than twice as many as had existed eight years earlier; they accounted for almost one-third of all the young nonwhites in the labor force.

The early years of the 1960s suffered a sudden and marked deterioration in certain key social indicators that, taken together, was unprecedented during any of the previous twenty or thirty years. Some of these indicators, such as teenage unemployment, were noticed and believed; others, such as those about crime and families, were noticed but not believed; and still others, such as that pertaining to heroin addiction, were scarcely even noticed. Or, more precisely, "informed opinion" did not notice or believe many of these indicators.

The price that we paid for this oversight—in confusion, frustration, and social divisions—was substantial. At the very time when the United States was embarking on its greatest period of sustained prosperity, a period that was to produce major improvements in the incomes, educational levels, and housing and health conditions of almost every major segment of our population, the quality of life, especially of life in public places, was rapidly worsening. We were achieving the Great Society

11

without producing the good life, enhancing our prosperity without improving our tranquillity.

The crucial years seem to have been 1962 and 1963. Well before the war in Vietnam had fully engaged us or the ghetto riots had absorbed us, the social bonds—the ties of family, of neighborhood, of mutual forbearance and civility—seem to have come asunder. Why?

That question should be, and no doubt in time will be, seriously debated. No single explanation, perhaps no set of explanations, will ever gain favor. One fact, however, is an obvious beginning to an explanation: by 1962 and 1963 there had come of age the persons born during the baby boom of the immediate postwar period. A child born in 1946 would have been sixteen in 1962, seventeen in 1963.

The numbers involved were very large. In 1950 there were about twenty-four million persons aged fourteen to twenty-four; by 1960 that had increased only slightly to just under twenty-seven million. But during the next ten years it increased by over thirteen million persons. Every year for ten years, the number of young people increased by 1.3 million. That ten-year increase was greater than the growth in the young segment of the population for the rest of the *century* put together. To state it in another way that focuses on the critical years of 1962 and 1963, during the first *two* years of the decade of the 1960s, we added more young persons (about 2.6 million) to our population than we had added in any preceding *ten* years since 1930.

The result of this has been provocatively stated by Professor Norman B. Ryder, the Princeton University demographer: "There is a perennial invasion of barbarians who must somehow be civilized and turned into contributors to fulfillment of the various functions requisite to societal survival." That "invasion" is the coming of age of a new generation of young people. Every society copes with this enormous socialization process more or less successfully, but occasionally that process is almost literally swamped by a quantitative discontinuity in the numbers of persons involved: "The increase in the magnitude of the socialization tasks in the United States during the past decade was completely outside the bounds of previous experience." [5]

If we continue Professor Ryder's metaphor, we note that in 1950 and still in 1960 the "invading army" (those aged fourteen to twenty-four) were outnumbered three to one by the size of the "defending army" (those aged twenty-five to sixty-four). By 1970 the ranks of the former had grown so fast that they were only outnumbered two to one by the latter, a state of affairs that had not existed since 1910.

The significance of these numbers can scarcely be exaggerated. They are best understood by looking at one city. Take Washington, D.C. It has a large black population, a high crime rate, and is the source of countless stories about popular fears of criminal attack and countless political speeches about the need to get tough. One would think that it is a city whose population deteriorated substantially in the last decade or two. In fact, by most measures, quite the opposite is the case.

Consider the black population, which is almost three-fourths of the total. Its median educational level increased from 8.8 years of schooling in 1950 to 11.4 years in 1970. [6] In 1950 there were only ten thousand black adults in the city with a college education; in 1970 there were twenty-two thousand. Black median family income, adjusted for inflation, tripled during the two decades. In 1970, when there was substantial unemployment in the country as a whole, the unemployment for black men aged twenty to fifty-nine in Washington was only 4.5 per cent, and for black women the same age it was even less—3.6 per cent. Washington has manifold problems of poor housing, poverty, and inadequate schooling, but it is not by any conceivable measure a vast lower-class slum or a city that has lost ground economically or educationally. To a substantial degree, it is a black middle-class or lower-middle-class community.

Yet Washington has for almost a decade been in the grip of a massive crime, heroin, and welfare problem. A large part of the reason is the change in that city's age structure. In 1960 there were about sixty-five thousand persons aged sixteen to twenty-one in the city. Ten years later, as the postwar baby boom left its mark, that number had risen to over eighty-six thousand—an increase of more than 30 per cent. During the 1930s there had been only about eight thousand live births each year in the city; by the end of World War II that number had risen to about twenty thousand per year.

The vast majority of these additional children entered the life of the city and its institutions just the way they had always done—they went to school, took jobs, got married, and had children of their own (though far fewer than the number of children their parents had). A small proportion of them did the rebellious things that some young people always do. But this time, it was a small proportion of a very large number.

The schools were among the first institutions to notice the change. The number of dropouts from Washington junior high schools began to increase beginning in 1962, and peaked in 1964.

Then, as the children got older, the number of dropouts from the senior high schools began to rise, peaking in 1968. When those in school or out of school started looking for jobs, they discovered that the number of new young applicants had increased far faster than the number of jobs. In Washington, the unemployment rate for blacks of ages sixteen to twenty-one had been around 8 per cent during the 1950s, but during the 1960s it rose steadily until it reached 16 per cent for males and 20 per cent for females by 1970.

The proportion of young males in Washington who became addicted to heroin before the 1960s had been, as best one can estimate it, less than 3 per cent. One might have expected that rate to remain the same for the new, larger population of young people coming of age in the 1960s. If it had, the number of addicts would have gone up by at least a third—a serious problem, to be sure, but nothing like the epidemic that actually struck. In fact, the addiction rate for males born in the decade following 1945 who grew up in Washington was over ten times the "normal" level. As the epidemic mounted, certain age groups were

14

devastated. Of the six thousand young Washington men born in 1953, over 13 per cent became heroin addicts, and in some areas of the city about one-fourth of the males born in that year became heroin users. In the single year 1969, about 5 per cent of the males sixteen years old became addicted to heroin.

Some women were becoming addicts as well, but in absolute and relative terms their numbers were far smaller than those of the male addicts. For young women, or a fraction of them, welfare rather than heroin led to their identification as a significant group. For several decades AFDC had been utilized principally by older women who had lost their husbands. In the 1960s, as large numbers of young women entered childbearing age, there was both an increase in AFDC utilization and a change in the kind of recipient. The women on AFDC in Washington tripled between 1961 and 1971, from five thousand to over sixteen thousand, and the largest growth occurred among young women. The number on AFDC who were over thirty increased by 140 per cent, but the number who were under thirty increased by 300 per cent, and the number who were under twenty increased by 800 per cent. In ten years, the age of the typical woman on AFDC fell from thirty to twenty-three.

Crime increased rapidly in this same period. Here, of course, even crude estimates of the number of young persons involved is very difficult. We obviously do not know the age of those who commit crimes, only the age of those arrested for crimes. And we do not know how many crimes are committed by the same person. But we can make some guesses, based on a recent study in Philadelphia that is perhaps the best analysis available of youthful crime. Professor Marvin Wolfgang and his coworkers at the University of Pennsylvania examined the delinquency records of all the males born in 1945 who lived in Philadelphia between their tenth and eighteenth birthdays.[7] They were able to find over ten thousand of them, and learned that more than one-third had at least one recorded contact with the police by the time they were eighteen, and half of these had more than one such contact. Of the delinquent acts recorded, perhaps a quarter could be regarded as relatively serious crimes. Most of the crimes were committed when the boys were fifteen, sixteen, or seventeen.

Suppose those proportions were true for Washington (they are not likely to be exactly the same, because the racial and economic composition of the cities differ). Since the number of persons aged sixteen to twenty-one increased by twenty-one thousand during the 1960s, and if one-third of these committed one or more delinquent acts, then by 1970 there were at least seven thousand more delinquents in the city than there had been when the decade started. Since each delinquent will have committed at least three offenses known to the police before he turns eighteen, twenty-one thousand more offenses resulting in an arrest were committed. There were no doubt many thousands more that did not produce a police contact.

Three aspects of these data are of paramount importance. One is that much (but not all) of the increase in crime, welfare utilization, and heroin addiction can be explained by the sheer numbers of young persons involved, without adducing any theory about the breakdown of the family, church, or society.

The second is that, except for heroin addiction during certain years in certain districts of the city, the young persons responsible for these behaviors were only a small minority of all the young persons. Dr. Robert Dupont estimates that of the 147,000 persons born in the decade after World War II who lived in Washington in the 1960s, about 17,200, or less than 12 per cent, were either on heroin or on welfare or both.

But the third is that changes in the age structure of the population cannot alone account for the social dislocations of the sixties. While the number of persons between the ages of sixteen and twenty-one in the District of Columbia increased by 32 per cent between 1960 and 1970, the social problems increased much more: the rate of serious crime went up by over 400 per cent, welfare rates by over 200 per cent, unemployment rates by at least 100 per cent, and heroin addiction by (a best guess) over

1,000 per cent. Detroit, to cite another example, had about one hundred murders in 1960 but over five hundred in 1971, yet the number of young persons did not quintuple.

A close study of murder rates in various cities has recently been carried out by Arnold Barnett and his associates at the Massachusetts Institute of Technology. They conclude that the increase in the murder rate during the 1960s was more than ten times greater than what one would have expected from the changing age structure of the population alone. Apparently much more complex forces are at work in almost all large cities. Though Detroit has become known, erroneously, as the "murder capital of the world" (actually, Atlanta enjoys that dubious distinction), the increase in the murder rate was roughly the same in the fifty largest cities—it about doubled between 1963 and 1971. Clearly, some broad national forces are involved, but exactly what they are, no one knows. The results, however, are chilling: If the murder rate holds constant at today's level, then a child born in 1974 in Detroit and living there all his life has a one in thirty-five chance of being murdered. And if the murder rate continues to increase at its present pace, his chances of meeting a felonious end increase to one *in fourteen*. At current levels, Barnett points out, a typical baby born and remaining in a large American city is more likely to die of murder than an American soldier in World War II was to die in combat. [8]

Other analyses confirm that the rise in crime rates in the 1960s was not wholly the simple result of an increase in the number of young persons in the population. Theodore Ferdinand calculated from published arrest figures that only 13.4 per cent of the increase in arrests for robbery between 1950 and 1965 could be accounted for by the increase in the number of persons between the ages of ten and twenty-four. [9]

One possibility is that the sudden increase in the number of persons at risk has an exponential effect on the rate of certain social problems. There is, perhaps, a "critical mass" of young

17

persons such that, when that number is reached, or when an increase in that mass is sudden and large, a self-sustaining chain reaction is set off that creates an explosive increase in the amount of crime, addiction, and welfare dependency.[10] What had once been relatively isolated and furtive acts (copping a fix, stealing a TV) become widespread and group-supported activities.

Heroin addiction is an example. We have had addicts since at least 1900, and we have always had young people who were potential addicts. We also know, as will be explained in Chapter 7, that addiction spreads like a contagion, with one friend turning on another. Yet ordinarily this contagion is rather contained and results in no epidemic of the sort that broke out in the 1960s. The sudden, dramatic increase in the number of potential addicts seems to have created a self-sustaining contagion that rapidly produced a more-than-proportional number of actual addicts.

At the same time, our society did a number of things that nurtured this reaction. The media spread the message that a "youth culture" was being born, and celebrated the cult of personal liberation that seemed to be central to that culture. Enhanced personal mobility made it easier to carry a contagion from one group to another. Social programs designed to combat poverty brought together groups that once would have been isolated from each other, and thus spread the contagion as surely as bringing men together in the Army during World War I spread the influenza epidemic. The contacts of upper-middle-class suburban youths with ghetto blacks as a result of civil rights programs increased access to the drug culture, or perhaps created in the eyes of the whites the mistaken view that such a "culture" existed, and was desirable, when in fact only deviant and episodic drug taking existed.

The institutional mechanisms which could handle problems in ordinary numbers were suddenly swamped, and may, in some cases, have broken down so fully as barely to function at all. The deterrent force of the police and the courts may not be great in normal times, but it may have declined absolutely, and not just relatively, in those exceptional times. The increase in crime produced a less-than-proportionate increase in arrests and, of those arrested, probably a less-than-proportionate increase in penalties. If the supply and value of legitimate opportunities (i.e., jobs) was declining at the very time that the cost of illegitimate activities (i.e., fines and jail terms) was also declining, a rational teenager might well have concluded that it made more sense to steal cars than to wash them.

One is tempted to ask, "What might have been?" If the age structure of the decade had been normal, if crime and addiction and welfare dependency had not increased so dramatically, could we have come to grips with our problems any more successfully than we did? Indeed, what would we have considered our problems to be? The war and its divisiveness would have occurred in any event. The demand by blacks for equality of opportunity would still have arisen, though the number of young blacks available for militant protest would have been smaller. The ghetto riots might still have occurred—just as it was hard beforehand to predict that they would occur, it is hard after the fact to predict the circumstances under which they would not have erupted.

But perhaps some problems would have been easier to address had not the social structure appeared to collapse. We might have had a more sensible discussion of riots and what to do about them if it had not been so easy for some to link (incorrectly, I think) the existence of rioting with the rise of ordinary criminality. Programs designed to solve teenage unemployment would clearly have been more successful if so large a fraction of the teenagers to be employed were not deeply involved in heroin addiction and remunerative crime. In retrospect, we might not have described certain "Great Society" programs as failures if the problems they sought to remedy—unemployment, school dropouts, low educational achievement—had not been suddenly enlarged in scope and altered in character. Rebuilding or rehabilitating our inner-city neighborhoods might well have been much easier under public auspices—indeed, might have occurred under private auspices—were not so many of these areas destroyed as communities by crime and addiction.

But we are not yet sure we can even explain what did happen; we shall never be able to explain what might have happened.

Chapter 2

Crime and Community

PREDATORY crime does not merely victimize individuals, it impedes and, in the extreme case, even prevents the formation and maintenance of community. By disrupting the delicate nexus of ties, formal and informal, by which we are linked with our neighbors, crime atomizes society and makes of its members mere individual calculators estimating their own advantage, especially their own chances for survival amidst their fellows. Common undertakings become difficult or impossible, except for those motivated by a shared desire for protection. (Coming together for protection may, of course, lead to a greater sense of mutual aid and dependence and provide the basis for larger and more positive commitments. It was out of a desire for self-defense, after all, that many of the earliest human settlements arose. But then it was a banding together against a common *external* enemy. Mutual protection against an enemy within is more difficult to achieve, less sustaining of a general sense of community, and more productive of conflict as disputes arise over who is victim and who the aggressor.)

It was the failure to appreciate the importance of community and the gravity of the threats to it that led to some mistaken views during the 1960s of the true nature of the "urban crisis." Until at least the latter half of that decade, we were told by leaders that the "key problem" facing our cities was, variously, inadequate transportation, declining retail sales, poor housing, or rising taxes. Though the average citizen no doubt shared these and other concerns in some measure, he was increasingly restive that his view of the problem of his city was not taken seriously.

This view was to be found in a number of opinion surveys but, until nearly the end of the decade, it was not taken seriously by many of those in charge of public policy for cities. There was a curious failure of representation in our political system for which I offer some explanations in Chapter 4. I first became aware of the gap between what people were saying and leaders were doing in 1966 when a colleague and I conducted a poll of over one thousand Boston homeowners. We asked what each respondent thought was the biggest problem facing the city. The "conventional" urban problems—housing, transportation, pollution, urban renewal, and so on—were a major concern of only 18 per cent of those questioned, and these were disproportionately the wealthier, better-educated respondents. Only 9 per cent mentioned jobs and employment, even though many of those interviewed had incomes at or below what is often regarded as the poverty level. The issue which concerned more respondents than any other was variously stated—crime, violence, rebellious youth, racial tension, public immorality, delinquency. However stated, the common theme seemed to be a concern for improper behavior in public places.

From some white respondents this was no doubt a covert way of indicating antiblack feelings. But it was not primarily that, for these same forms of impropriety were mentioned more often than other problems by black respondents as well. And those among the whites who indicated, in answer to another question, that they felt the government ought to do more to help blacks were just as likely to mention impropriety as those who felt the government had already done too much.

Nor was this pattern peculiar to Boston. A survey done for *Fortune* magazine in which over three hundred black males were questioned in thirteen major cities showed similar results.[1] In this study, people were not asked what was the biggest problem of their city, but rather what was the biggest problem they faced as individuals. When stated this generally, it was not surprising that jobs and education were given the highest priority. What is striking is that close behind came the same "urban" problems found in Boston—a concern for crime, violence, the need for more police protection, and so on. Indeed, these issues ranked ahead of the expressed desire for a higher income. Surveys reported by the President's Commission on Law Enforcement and Administration of Justice showed crime and violence ranking high as major problems among both black and white respondents.[2] Today, of course, the importance of crime as a public concern is well known. Eight or ten years ago, for reasons set forth in Chapter 4, this concern was either denied or ignored. And even today, a concern for crime remains, to some, an indication of a "conservative" inclination despite the fact that the victims of crimes are disproportionately to be found in communities (or increasingly, noncommunities) that support liberal candidates.

The Failure of Community

IN READING the responses to the Boston survey, I was struck by how various and general were the ways of expressing public concern in this area. "Crime in the streets" was not the stock answer, though that came up often enough. Indeed, many of the forms of impropriety mentioned involved little that was criminal in any serious sense—rowdy teenagers, for example, or various indecencies (lurid advertisements in front of neighborhood movies and racy paperbacks in the local drugstore).

What these concerns have in common, and thus what constitutes the "urban problem" for a large percentage (perhaps a majority) of urban citizens, is a sense of the failure of community. By "community" I do not mean, as some do, a metaphysical entity or abstract collectivity with which people "need" to affiliate. There may be an "instinct" for "togetherness" arising out of ancient or tribal longings for identification, but different people gratify it in different ways, and for most the gratification has little to do with neighborhood or urban conditions. When I speak of the concern for "community," I refer to a desire for the observance of standards of right and seemly conduct in the public places in which one lives and moves, those standards to be consistent with—and supportive of—the values and life styles of the particular individual.[3] Around one's home, the places where one shops, and the corridors through which one walks there is for each of us a public space wherein our sense of security, self-esteem, and propriety is either reassured or jeopardized by the people and events we encounter. Viewed this way, the concern for community is less the "need" for "belonging" (or, in equally vague language, the "need" to overcome feelings of "alienation" or "anomie") than the normal but not compulsive interest of any rationally self-interested person in his and his family's environment.

A rationally self-interested person would, I argue, take seriously those things which affect him most directly and importantly and over which he feels he can exercise the greatest influence. Next to one's immediate and particular needs for such things as shelter, income, and education, one's social and physical surroundings have perhaps the greatest consequence for oneself and one's family. Furthermore, unlike those city-wide or national forces which influence a person, what happens to him at the neighborhood level is most easily affected by his own actions. The way he behaves will, ideally, alter the behavior of others; the remarks he makes and the way he presents himself and his home will shape, at least marginally, the common expectations by which the appropriate standards of public conduct in that area are determined. How he dresses, how loudly or politely he speaks, how well he trims his lawn or paints his house, the liberties he permits his children to enjoy—all those not only express what the individual thinks is appropriate conduct, but in some degree influence what his neighbors take to be appropriate conduct.

Controlling the Immediate Environment

IT IS primarily at the neighborhood level that meaningful (i.e., potentially rewarding) opportunities for the exercise of urban citizenship exist. And it is the breakdown of neighborhood controls (neighborhood self-government, if you will) that accounts for the principal concerns of many urban citizens. When they can neither take for granted nor influence by their actions and those of their neighbors the standards of conduct within their own neighborhood community, they experience what to them are "urban problems"—problems that arise directly out of the unmanageable consequences of living in close proximity.

I suspect that this concern for the maintenance of the neighborhood community explains in part the overwhelming preference Americans have for small cities and towns. According to a Gallup Poll taken in 1963, only 22 per cent of those interviewed wanted to live in cities, 49 per cent preferred small towns, and 28 per cent preferred suburbs. (Only among blacks, interestingly enough, did a majority prefer large cities—perhaps because the costs of rural or small town life, in terms of poverty and discrimination, are greater for the black than the costs, in terms of disorder and insecurity, of big city life.) Small towns and suburbs, because they are socially more homogeneous than large cities and because local self-government can be used to reinforce informal neighborhood sanctions, apparently make the creation and maintenance of a proper sense of community easier. At any rate, Americans are acting on this preference for small places, whatever its basis. As Daniel Elazar has pointed out, the smaller cities are claiming a growing share of the population; the largest cities are not increasing in size at all, and some, indeed, are getting smaller.[4]

A rational concern for community implies a tendency to behave in certain ways which some popular writers have mistakenly thought to be the result of conformity, prejudice, or an excessive concern for appearances. No doubt all of these factors play some role in the behavior of many people and a dominant role in the behavior of a few, but one need not make any such assumptions to explain the nature of most neighborhood conduct. In dealing with one's immediate environment under circumstances that make individual actions efficacious in constraining the actions of others, one will develop a range of sanctions to employ against others, and will, in turn, respond to the sanctions that others use. Such sanctions are typically informal, even casual, and may consist of little more than a gesture, word, or expression. Occasionally direct action is taken—a complaint, or even making a scene—but resort to these measures is rare because they invite counterattacks ("If that's the way he feels about it, I'll just show him!") and because, if used frequently, they lose their effectiveness. The purpose of the sanctions is to regulate the external consequences of private behavior—to handle, in the language of economists, "third-party effects," "externalities," and "the production of collective goods." I may wish to let my lawn go to pot, but one ugly lawn affects the appearance of the whole neighborhood, just as one sooty incinerator smudges clothes that others have hung out to dry. Rowdy children raise the noise level and tramp down the flowers for everyone, not just for their parents.

Because the sanctions employed are subtle, informal, and

delicate, not everyone is equally vulnerable to everyone else's discipline. Furthermore, if there is not a generally shared agreement as to appropriate standards of conduct, these sanctions will be inadequate to correct such deviations as occur. A slight departure from a norm is set right by a casual remark; a commitment to a different norm is very hard to alter, unless, of course, the deviant party is "eager to fit in," in which case he is not committed to the different norm at all but simply looking for signs as to what the preferred norms may be. Because of these considerations, the members of a community have a general preference for social homogeneity and a suspicion of heterogeneity—a person different in one respect (e.g., income, race, or speech) may be different in other respects as well (e.g., how much noise or trash he is likely to produce).

Prejudice and Diversity

THIS REASONING sometimes leads to error—people observed to be outwardly different may not in fact behave differently, or such differences in behavior as exist may be irrelevant to the interests of the community. Viewed one way, these errors are exceptions to rule-of-thumb guides or empirical generalizations; viewed another way, they are manifestations of prejudice. And in fact one of the unhappiest complexities of the logic of neighborhood is that it can so often lead one wrongly to impute to another person some behavioral problem on the basis of the latter's membership in a racial or economic group. Even worse, under cover of acting in the interests of the neighborhood, some people may give vent to the most unjustified and neurotic prejudices.

However much we may regret such expressions of prejudice, it does little good to imagine that the occasion for their expression can be wished away. We may even pass laws (as I think we should) making it illegal to use certain outward characteristics (like race) as grounds for excluding people from a neighborhood. But the core problem will remain—owing to the importance of community to most people, and given the process whereby new arrivals are inducted into and constrained by the sanctions of the neighborhood, the suspicion of heterogeneity will only be overcome when a person proves by his actions that his distinctive characteristic is not a sign of any disposition to violate the community's norms.

Such a view seems to be at odds with the notion that the big city is the center of cosmopolitanism—by which is meant, among other things, diversity. And so it is. A small fraction of the population (in my judgment, a very small fraction) may want diversity so much that it will seek out the most cosmopolitan sections of the cities as places to live. Some of these people are intellectuals, others are young, unmarried persons with a taste for excitement before assuming the responsibilities of a family, and still others are "misfits" who have dropped out of society for a variety of reasons. Since one element of this group—the intellectuals—writes the books which define the "urban problem," we are likely to be confused by their preferences and assume that the problem is in part to maintain the heterogeneity and cosmopolitanism of the central city—to attract and hold a neat balance among middle-class families, young culture-lovers, lower-income blacks, "colorful" Italians, and big businessmen. To assume this is to mistake the preferences of the few for the needs of the many. And even the few probably exaggerate just how much diversity they wish. Manhattan intellectuals are often as worried about crime in the streets as their cousins in Queens. The desired diversity is "safe" diversity—a harmless variety of specialty stores, esoteric bookshops, "ethnic" restaurants, and highbrow cultural enterprises. I suspect that the tolerance for social diversity, especially "safe" diversity, increases with education and decreases with age. This tolerance, however, does not extend to "unsafe" diversity—street crime, for example.

On "Middle-Class Values"

AT THIS POINT I had better take up explicitly the dark thoughts forming in the minds of some readers that this analysis is little more than an elaborate justification for prejudice, philistinism, conformity, and (worst of all) "middle-class values." The number of satirical books on suburbs seems to suggest that the creation of a sense of community is at best little more than enforcing the lowest common denominator of social behavior by means of kaffee klatsches and the exchange of garden tools; at worst, it is the end of privacy and individuality and the beginning of discrimination in its uglier forms.

I have tried to deal with the prejudice argument above. Prejudice exists, as does the desire for community; both often overlap. There is no "solution" to the problem, though stigmatizing certain kinds of prejudgments (such as those based on race) is helpful. Since (in my opinion) social class is the primary basis (with age and religion not far behind) on which community-maintaining judgments are made, and since social class (again, in my opinion) is a much better predictor of behavior than race, I foresee the time when racial distinctions will be much less salient (though never absent) in handling community problems. Indeed, much of what passes for "race prejudice" today may be little more than class prejudice, with race used as a rough indicator of approximate social class.

With respect to the charge of defending "middle-class values," let me stress that the analysis of "neighborhood" offered here makes no assumptions about the substantive values enforced by the communal process. On the contrary, the emphasis is on the process itself; in principle, it could be used to enforce any set of values. To be sure, we most often observe it enforcing the injunctions against noisy children and lawns infested with crabgrass, but I suppose it could also be used to enforce injunctions against turning children into "sissies" and being enslaved by lawn-maintenance chores. In fact, if we turn our attention to the city and end our preoccupation with suburbia, we will find many kinds of neighborhoods with a great variety of substantive values being enforced. Jane Jacobs described how and to what ends informal community controls operate in working-class Italian sections of New York and elsewhere. Middle-class black neighborhoods tend also to develop a distinctive code. And Bohemian or "hippie" sections (despite their loud disclaimers of any interest in either restraint or constraint) establish and sustain a characteristic ethos.

People without Communities

VIEWED historically, the process whereby neighborhoods, in the sense intended in this chapter, have been formed in the large cities might be thought of as one in which order arose out of chaos to return in time to a new form of disorder.

Immigrants, thrust together in squalid central-city ghettos, gradually worked their way out to establish, first with the aid of streetcar lines and then with the aid of automobiles, more or less homogeneous and ethnically distinct neighborhoods of single-family and two-family houses. In the Boston survey, the average respondent had lived in his present neighborhood for about twenty years. When asked what his neighborhood had been like when he was growing up, the vast majority of those questioned said that it was "composed of people pretty much like myself"— similar, that is, in income, ethnicity, religion, and so on. In time, of course, families—especially those of childrearing age— began spilling out over the city limits into the suburbs, and were replaced in the central city by persons lower in income than themselves.

Increasingly, the central city is coming to be made up of persons who have no interest, or who face special disabilities, in creating and maintaining a sense of community. There are several such groups, each with a particular problem and each with varying degrees of ability to cope with that problem. One is composed of affluent whites without children (young couples, single persons, elderly couples whose children have left home) who either (as with the "young swingers") lack an interest in community or (as with the elderly couples) lack the ability to participate meaningfully in the maintenance of community. But for such persons there are alternatives to community—principally, the occupancy of a special physical environment that in effect insulates the occupant from such threats as it is the function of community to control. They move into high-rise buildings in which their apartment is connected by an elevator to either a basement garage (where they can step directly into their car) or to a lobby guarded by a doorman and perhaps even a private police force. Thick walls and high fences protect such open spaces as exist from the intrusion of outsiders. The apartments may even be air-conditioned, so that the windows need never be opened to admit street noises. Interestingly, a common complaint of such apartment-dwellers is that, in the newer buildings at least, the walls are too thin to ensure privacy—in short, the one failure of the physical substitute for community occasions the major community-oriented complaint.

A second group of noncommunal city residents are the poor whites, often elderly, who financially or for other reasons are unable to leave the old central-city neighborhood when it changes character. For many, that change is the result of the entry of blacks or Puerto Ricans into the block, and this gives rise to the number of antiblack or anti-Puerto Rican remarks which an interviewer encounters. But sometimes the neighborhood is taken over by young college students, or by artists, or by derelicts; then the remarks are antiyouth, antistudent, antiartist, or antidrunk. The fact that the change has instituted a new and (to the older resident) less seemly standard of conduct is more important than the attributes of the persons responsible for the change. Elderly persons, because they lack physical vigor and the access to neighbors which having children facilitates,

31

are especially vulnerable to neighborhood changes and find it especially difficult to develop substitutes for community—except, of course, to withdraw behind locked doors and drawn curtains. They cannot afford the high-rise buildings and private security guards that are the functional equivalent of communal sanctions for the wealthier city dweller.

In the Boston survey, the fear of impropriety and violence was highest for those respondents who were the oldest and the poorest. Preoccupation with such issues as the major urban problem was greater among women than among men, among those over sixty-five years of age than among those under, among Catholics than among Jews, and among those earning less than $5,000 a year than among those earning higher incomes. (Incidentally, these were not the same persons most explicitly concerned about and hostile to blacks—antiblack sentiment was more common among middle-aged married couples who had children and modestly good incomes.)

Though the elderly may be more preoccupied with crime and violence than are those who are younger, they are not more likely to be victimized by it. In 1973 the Law Enforcement Assistance Administration (LEAA) of the Department of Justice sponsored a survey by the Census Bureau of about fifty thousand households in the five largest cities. In four of the five cities, persons over the age of fifty were much less likely to be the victim of a robbery than those under fifty, and in all five cities they were much less likely to be the victim of a burglary.[5]

The third group specially afflicted by the perceived breakdown of community are the blacks. For them, residential segregation as well as other factors have led to a condition in which there is relatively little spatial differentiation among blacks of various class levels. Lower-class, working-class, and middle-class blacks are squeezed into close proximity in such a way as to inhibit or prevent the territorial separation necessary for the creation and maintenance of different communal life styles. Segregation in the housing market is probably much more intense with respect to lower-cost housing than with middle-cost housing, suggesting that middle-class blacks may find it easier to move into previously all-white neighborhoods. But the constricted supply of low-cost housing means that a successful invasion of a new area by middle-class blacks often leads to their being followed rather quickly by those of the working and lower classes. As a result, unless middle-class blacks can leapfrog out to distant white (or new) communities, they will find themselves struggling to assert hegemony over a territory threatened on several sides by blacks with quite different life styles.

The black population has become residentially more, not less, segregated in the past ten or twenty years. A Census Bureau survey of twenty large cities found that the proportion of blacks living in census tracts that were three-fourths or more black increased from 36 per cent in 1960 to 50 per cent in 1970.[6] Though there has been some black migration to the suburbs, the proportion of blacks in metropolitan areas who live in the central cities has actually risen from 77 per cent in 1960 to 79 per cent in 1970. During this period of increasing residential concentration, the material conditions of black life have generally improved; there have been dramatic gains in real income, housing quality, and educational attainment. Some of the members of the growing black middle class have been able to escape the inner city, but most have not.

This has meant that efforts by blacks to assert and defend a sense of community have been frustrated by their inability to maintain some degree of territorial homogeneity. The territories they occupy have instead been quite heterogeneous—criminals and noncriminals, addicts and nonaddicts, the middle class and the lower class live in close proximity, even side by side. The creation of a middle-class community requires that middle-class values dominate, and this applies with equal force—perhaps with special force—to blacks. If a family sends its children to schools in which many students reject school work, if they live in an area where illegitimacy is as common as marriage, if they regularly encounter on the streets persons for whom self-expression is more attractive than self-control, the family will either

33

find itself conforming to a standard it does not value or isolating itself from its neighbors in ways that reduce even further such influence as that family might have on the behavior of others.

The residential isolation of blacks of various class levels in the central cities is a deeply destructive social phenomenon. As both Sar Levitan and Thomas Sowell have observed, the dominant ethic of many inner-city areas is established by a lower class from which the working class and the middle class cannot escape, and which they cannot publicly repudiate without giving aid and comfort to whites who wish to believe the worst about blacks.[7] Furthermore, it has become fashionable in some quarters to argue that to be "truly black" is incompatible with being middle class; thus the canons of racial pride can lead many families to act other than as their own interests dictate and as the maintenance of community requires. In the long term, of course, racial pride—"black power"—may provide the common sense of self-respect out of which a new and strong sense of community can be forged. No one knows. In the short run, however, many middle-class black families are left with the unhappy choice between despair and rage.

The LEAA survey cited earlier confirms the greater likelihood of black victimization. In all five of the largest cities, blacks are much more likely than whites to be the victims of robbery and burglary, in some cases by a ratio of nearly two to one. In four of the five cities, they are more likely to be the victims of aggravated assault. It is also generally the case that the very poorest persons, regardless of race, are more likely than the better off to be victims of a robbery. The reverse tends to be true of burglary, auto theft, and larceny. Perhaps robbery, a crime that depends on threats rather than stealth, is more likely to be committed by persons close to their own neighborhoods where escape is easy, whereas burglars, who operate unobserved, are more inclined to range over a wider territory in search of promising victims. Auto thieves, of course, steal autos from those who own them, and therefore the victims are in general affluent.

It is often said that the greatest price of segregation is the perpetuation of a divided society, one black and the other white. While there is some merit in this view, it overlooks the fact that most ethnic groups, when reasonably free to choose a place to live, have chosen to live among people similar to themselves. (I am thinking especially of the predominantly Jewish suburbs.) The real price of segregation, in my opinion, is not that it forces blacks and whites apart but that it forces blacks of different class positions together. A black writer, Orde Coombs, has vividly portrayed the despair and terror that has come to be the daily lot of the residents of Harlem, and, no doubt, of many other ghettos. The streets are no longer controlled by either the respectable residents or by the police, but by the members of an "underclass" who "viciously prey upon the weak, the old, and the unsuspecting," for whom fear is "something palpable that walks among us every day and will not leave us alone." [8]

What City Government Cannot Do

COMMUNAL social controls tend to break down either when persons with an interest in, and the competence for, maintaining a community no longer live in the area, or when they remain but their neighborhood is not sufficiently distinct, territorially, from areas with different or threatening life styles. In the latter case especially, the collapse of informal social controls leads to demands for the imposition of formal or institutional controls—demands for "more police protection," more or better public services, and so on. The difficulty, however, is that there is relatively little government can do directly to maintain a neighborhood community. It can, of course, assign more police officers to it, but, as suggested in Chapters 5 and 6, there are limits to the effectiveness of this response. For one thing, a city has only so many officers, and those assigned to one neighborhood must often be taken away from another. Perhaps more important, the police can rarely manage all relevant aspects of conduct in public places, whatever may be their success in handling serious crime (such as muggings). Juvenile rowdiness, quarrels among neighbors, landlord-tenant disputes, the unpleasant side effects of a well-patronized tavern—all these are matters which may be annoying enough to warrant police intervention but not to warrant arrests. Managing these kinds of public disorder is a common task for the police, but one that they can rarely manage to everyone's satisfaction—precisely because the disorder arises out of a dispute among residents over what ought to be the standard of proper conduct.

City governments, during the 1950s and early 1960s, became increasingly remote from neighborhood concerns. Partly this was the consequence of the growing centralization of local government—mayors were getting stronger at the expense of city councils, city-wide organizations (such as newspapers and civic associations) were getting stronger at the expense of neighborhood-based political parties, and new "superagencies" were being created in city hall to handle such matters as urban renewal, public welfare, and antipoverty programs. Mayors and citizens in many cities have begun to react against this trend and to search for ways of reinvolving government in neighborhood concerns; officials are setting up "little city halls," going on walking tours of their cities, and meeting with neighborhood and block clubs. But there is a limit to how effective such responses can be, because whatever the institutional structure, the issues that most concern a neighborhood are typically those about which politicians can do relatively little.

These issues involve disputes among the residents of a neighborhood, or between the residents of two adjoining neighborhoods, and the mayor takes sides in these matters—such as busing—only at his peril. Many of the issues involve no tangible stake; they concern more the quality of life and competing standards of propriety and less the dollars-and-cents value of particular services or programs. Officials with experience in organizing little city halls or police-community relations programs often report that a substantial portion (perhaps a majority) of the complaints they receive concern people who "don't keep up their houses," or who "let their children run wild," or who "have noisy parties." Sometimes the city can do something (e.g., by sending building inspectors to look over a house that appears to be a firetrap or by having the health department require that someone clean up a lot he has littered), but just as often the city can do little except offer its sympathy.

Poverty, Race, and Community

INDIRECTLY, and especially over the long run, government can do much more. First and foremost, it can help persons enter into those social classes wherein the creation and maintenance of community is easiest. Lower-class persons (by definition, I would argue) attach little importance to the opinions of others; they are preoccupied with the daily struggle for survival and the immediate gratifications that may be attendant on survival and are inclined to uninhibited, expressive conduct. A lower-*income* person, of course, is not necessarily lower *class*; the former condition reflects how much money he has, while the latter indicates the attitudes he possesses. Programs designed to increase prosperity and end poverty (defined as having too little money) will enable lower-income persons who care about the opinions of others to leave areas populated by lower-income persons who don't care (that is, areas populated by lower-class persons).

Governments and private organizations should continue to insure that, by law and in fact, citizens are not barred from moving from one neighborhood to another or from one community to another on grounds of race. To limit the housing opportunities available to blacks and other minorities to inner-city areas is to deny these people, on grounds other than their per-

37

sonal behavior, a chance to participate in or create for themselves a viable communal order.

In fact, there has been a dramatic increase in the number of persons who are middle class, and a substantial (though not dramatic) increase in the number of blacks who have been able to move out of inner-city or slum areas. Those who have benefited from these social changes have for the most part enhanced their personal safety and community tranquillity. But we must recognize that, in the short run at least, the areas left behind by this migration have often been made worse off, not because those who remained behind in the slums and deteriorating neighborhoods found themselves suddenly earning less money or living in worse housing, but because the human infrastructure of their communities had departed.

Many of those who once headed the block clubs, ran the PTAs, complained of poor garbage collection, manned the neighborhood political apparatus, and kept the streets under some degree of surveillance had moved out. They left a void, sometimes literally a physical one. The growing number of abandoned buildings in the central parts of New York and other cities is grim evidence of the reduction in population densities and the increased purchasing power of former slum-dwellers.

With the more affluent having departed and the community-maintenance functions they once served now undermanned, the rates of predatory crime in inner-city areas rose. At the same time, because some of those persons who moved out, white and black, were not yet by the standards of their new communities fully middle class, the reported rates of crime in these areas also went up. Hence the development of the (mislabeled) phenomenon, "suburban crime." It is not so much that "the suburbs" (by which we usually mean middle-class white suburbs) are becoming more criminal, but that the population of the various kinds of suburbs is changing.

If this line of argument is correct—and I stress that the social process I have just described is based on informed conjecture but not on established fact—then the population migrations from city to suburb, made possible by rising incomes and lessening racial barriers, have created conditions that contribute to the apparent paradox of rising crime rates in a period of prosperity.

The conversion of monetary prosperity into strong communal values is neither a simple nor quick process. But it would be as great a mistake to suppose that it is not happening at all as to suppose that it can happen overnight. After the Civil War, this country, in a feast of prosperity, personal liberation, and internal migration, accompanied by a rapid growth in the youthful segment of the population, experienced a wave of predatory crime unlike anything seen before or since. By the end of the century the jails and poorhouses were filled with Irishmen (probably including some ancestor of mine), and demands were heard for an end to immigration. Within a few decades, however, the crime rates had fallen dramatically as acculturation worked its way. There is as yet no reason to suppose that this process will not also operate in the decades ahead.

PART

II

THINKING
ABOUT CRIME

Chapter 3

Criminologists

THE "social science view" of crime is thought by many, especially its critics, to assert that crime is the result of poverty, racial discrimination, and other privations, and that the only morally defensible and substantively efficacious strategy for reducing crime is to attack its "root causes" with programs that end poverty, reduce discrimination, and meliorate privation. Certainly this is in part the view of President Johnson's Commission on Crime and Administration of Justice [1] and emphatically that of former Attorney General Ramsey Clark. [2] Both the former's report and the latter's book seemed to draw heavily on social science theories and findings.

Such a theory, if it is generally held by social scientists professionally concerned with crime, ought to be subjected to the closest scrutiny, because what it implies about the nature of man and society are of fundamental significance. Scholars would bear a grave responsibility if, by their theoretical and empirical work, they had supplied public policy with the assumption that men are driven primarily by the objective conditions in which they find themselves. Such a view might be correct, but it would first have to be reconciled with certain obvious objections—for example, that the crime rate in this country is higher than that in many other countries despite the fact that the material well-being of even the lowest stratum of our population is substantially greater than that of a comparable stratum in countries with much lower crime rates, or that crime rates have increased greatly during the very period (1963 to 1970) when there were great advances made in the income, schooling, and housing of almost all segments of society.

In fact, social scientists had not, at the time when their views on crime were sought by policy makers (roughly, the mid-1960s), set forth in writing a systematic theory of this sort. I asked three distinguished criminologists to nominate the two or three scholarly books on crime which were in print by mid-1960 and were then regarded as the most significant works on the subject. There was remarkable agreement as to the titles: *Principles of Criminology*, by Edwin H. Sutherland and Donald R. Cressey, and *Delinquency and Opportunity*, by Richard A. Cloward and Lloyd E. Ohlin, were most frequently cited.[3] Other works, including articles and symposia, were mentioned, and no claim was made that there was complete agreement on the validity of the views expressed in these books. Quite the contrary; criminologists then and now debate hotly and at length over such issues as "the cause of crime." But these two books are alike in the way questions are posed, answers sought, and policies derived—alike, in short, not in their specific theories of delinquency, but in the general perspective from which those theories flow. And this perspective, contrary to popular impression, has rather little to do with poverty, race, education, housing, or the other objective conditions that supposedly "cause" crime.

It is the argument of this chapter that in the mid-1960s, and perhaps today as well, social scientists concerned with crime shared a common perspective, but not one that emphasized the material condition of society; that this shared perspective led to a policy stalemate and an ethical dilemma; that when social scientists were asked for advice by national policy-making bodies, they could not respond with suggestions derived from and supported by their scholarly work; and that as a consequence such advice as was supplied tended to derive from their general political views as modified by their political and organizational interaction with those policy groups and their staffs.

This is a large argument, each step of which would require for its support substantial research and a lengthy paper. I have not done that research nor do I intend to write all those papers. Here I can only explain the reasoning behind the argument and show that a close reading of the relevant texts is consistent with it. I can also draw on the experiences of some criminologists who have worked with both the crime commission and the violence commission and who have recently written their reflections on that relationship.

The Criminological Perspective

THE TREATISE by Sutherland and Cressey is widely viewed as the leading text on the subject of crime. Its seventh edition appeared in 1966, just after President Johnson appointed his crime commission. Professor Lloyd Ohlin, an associate director of the commission's staff, has testified to the impact of many of the book's ideas on the work of the commission.[4]

The central theme of *Principles of Criminology* is that "criminal behavior results from the same social processes as other social behavior."[5] The task of the student of crime is twofold: to show how crime varies with social structure and social processes (e.g., how it is influenced by class, neighborhood, mobility, or density) and to explain how persons are inducted into crime (e.g., social imitation, "differential association," or attitude formation). Sutherland and Cressey review various perspectives on crime (or "schools of criminology") but fault all but the "sociological" approach. The "classical" theories of

Bentham and Beccaria are rejected because their underlying psychological assumption—that individuals calculate the pains and pleasures of crime and pursue it if the latter outweigh the former—"assumes freedom of the will in a manner which gives little or no possibility of further investigation of the causes of crime or of efforts to prevent crime." The hedonistic psychology suffers from being "individualistic, intellectualistic, and voluntaristic." [6] All "modern" schools of crime, Sutherland and Cressey suggest, reject this perspective and accept instead "the hypothesis of natural causation," by which they appear to mean that all other theories assume that crime is to some degree determined beyond the capacity of the individual freely, or at least easily, to resist.

Theories based on body type, mental abnormality, or mental illness are rejected because the available data are inconsistent with them. Criminals are no more likely than law-abiding persons to have a certain stature, to be feeble-minded, or to suffer from a psychosis. In the few brief pages devoted to alternatives to the sociological approach, it is striking that the argument that individuals choose crime freely because it is profitable is rejected on *theoretical* grounds, whereas those claiming that individuals are compelled toward crime, or at least made particularly susceptible to it, are rejected for *empirical* reasons. Nor are theoretical objections to the "classical" or "individualistic" perspective developed beyond the revealing statement that such a perspective forecloses the search for the causes of crime because it denies that crime is "caused."

There are, of course, many sociological theories of the causes of crime. Sutherland and Cressey prefer one, the "theory of differential association," but they (or rather Cressey, since Sutherland died before publication of this edition) do not insist that it has been established beyond dispute. We need not dwell on the details of "differential association," however, for its essential premises are not radically different from those of rival sociological theories—namely, that criminal behavior is learned by a person in intimate interaction with others whose good opinion he values, and that this learning places him in "normative conflict" with the larger society.

Sutherland and Cressey do not claim that poverty or racial discrimination cause crime, though crime may be higher in poor or segregated areas. Their references to the impact of poverty, defined as having little money, are few and skeptical. Sutherland is quoted from his earlier writings as observing that while crime is strongly correlated with geographic concentrations of poor persons, it is weakly correlated (if at all) with the economic cycle. That is, crime may be observed to increase as one enters a poor neighborhood, but it is not observed to increase as neighborhoods generally experience a depression, or to decrease as they experience prosperity. "Poverty as such," Sutherland concludes, "is not an important cause of crime." [7]

Being a member of a minority group and experiencing the frustrations produced by discrimination cannot explain crime for Sutherland and Cressey; while the experience of blacks, whose crime rate is high, might support such a theory, that of the Japanese, whose crime rate is low, refutes it. [8] Poverty and racial segregation may serve to perpetuate crime, however, to the extent that these factors prevent persons from leaving areas where crime is already high and thus from escaping those personal contacts and peer groups from which criminal habits are learned. Furthermore, Albert K. Cohen (to whom Sutherland and Cressey refer, approvingly) has shown that much of the delinquency found among working-class boys is "non-utilitarian"—that is, consists of expressive but financially unrewarding acts of vandalism and "hell-raising"—and that these acts are more common among this group than among middle-class boys. [9] If economic want were the cause of crime, one would predict that delinquency for gain would be more common among those less well-off, and delinquency for "fun" more common among the better-off, but the opposite seems to be the case.

There were other major theories of crime in 1966 in addition to those of Sutherland and Cressey. Most of these are reviewed in their treatise, and though criticisms are sometimes made, the governing assumptions of each are quite compatible with what the authors describe as the sociological approach. Sheldon and Eleanor Glueck, for example, produced in the 1950s a major effort to predict delinquency. While the idea of predicting delinquency became controversial on grounds of both fairness and feasibility, their empirical data on factors that helped "cause" delinquency were not seriously challenged. They argued and supplied data to show that among the key variables distinguishing delinquents from nondelinquents (holding age, neighborhood, and intelligence constant) are those related to family conditions, chiefly stability, parental affection, and the discipline of children.[10] Walter B. Miller has argued that delinquency is in large part an expression of the focal concerns of lower-class youth. Toughness, masculinity, "smartness," the love of excitement, and a desire for personal autonomy are valued by lower-class persons to a greater degree than by middle-class ones, and acting on the basis of these values, which are maintained by street-corner gangs, inevitably places many lower-class boys (and some girls) in conflict with the laws of the middle class.[11] Albert K. Cohen suggested that delinquency is in part the result of lower-class youth striving, not simply to assert their focal values, but to repudiate those middle-class values which they secretly prize.[12]

These and other sociological theories of crime, widely known and intensely discussed in the 1960s, have certain features in common. All seek to explain the "causes" of delinquency, or at least its persistence. All make attitude formation a key variable. All stressed that these attitudes are shaped and supported by intimate groups—the family and close friends. All were serious, intelligent efforts at constructing social theories, and while no theory was proved empirically, all were consistent with at least some important observations about crime. *But none could supply a plausible basis for the advocacy of public policy.*

This was true for several reasons. By directing attention toward the subjective states that preceded or accompanied criminal behavior, the sociological (or more accurately, social-psychological) theories directed attention toward conditions that cannot be easily and deliberately altered. Society, of course, shapes attitudes and values by its example, its institutions, and its practices, but slowly and imprecisely, and with great difficulty. If families inculcate habits of virtue, law-abidingness, and decorum, it is rarely because the family is acting as the agent of society or its government, but rather because it is a good family. If schools teach children to value learning and to study well, it is not simply because the schools are well-designed or generously supplied, but because attitudes consistent with learning and study already exist in the pupils. One may wonder what government might do if it wished to make good families even better or successful pupils even more successful: more resources might be offered to reduce burdens imposed by want, but the gains, if any, would probably be at the margin.

If it is hard by plan to make the good better, it may be impossible to make the bad tolerable so long as one seeks to influence attitudes and values directly. If a child is delinquent because his family made him so or his friends encourage him to be so, it is hard to conceive what society might do about his attitudes. No one knows how a government might restore affection, stability, and fair discipline to a family that rejects these characteristics; still less can one imagine how even a family once restored could affect a child who has passed the formative years and in any event has developed an aversion to one or both of his parents.

If the lower class has focal concerns that make crime attractive or even inevitable, it is not clear how government would supply "the lower class" with a new set of values consistent with law-abidingness. Indeed, the very effort to inculcate new values would, if the sociological theory is true, lead the members of that class to resist such alien intrusions all the more vigorously and to cling to their own world-view all the more strongly. One could supply the lower class with more money, of course, but if a class exists because of its values rather than its income, it is hard to see how, in terms of the prevailing theory, increasing the latter would improve the former.

Peer groups exist, especially for young people, as a way of defending their members from an alien, hostile, or indifferent larger society, and for supplying their members with a mutually satisfactory basis for self-respect. A deviant peer group—one that encourages crime or hell raising—would regard any effort by society to "reform" it as confirmation of the hostile intent of society and the importance of the group. For the members of a group to believe in a "we," they must believe in the existence of a "they"; the more a "they" asserts its difference or superiority, the more important the "we" is likely to become.

The problem lies in confusing causal analysis with policy analysis. Causal analysis attempts to find the source of human activity in those factors which themselves are not caused—which are, in the language of sociologists, "independent variables." Obviously nothing can be a cause if it is in turn caused by something else; it would then only be an "intervening variable." But ultimate causes cannot be the object of policy efforts precisely because, being ultimate, they cannot be changed. For example, criminologists have shown beyond doubt that men commit more crimes than women and younger men more (of certain kinds) than older ones. It is a theoretically important and scientifically correct observation. Yet it means little for policy makers concerned with crime prevention, since men cannot be changed into women or made to skip over the adolescent years. Not every primary cause is itself unchangeable; the cause of air pollution is (in part) certain gases in automobile exhausts, and thus reducing those gases by redesigning the engine will reduce pollution. But social problems—that is to say, problems occasioned by human behavior rather than mechanical processes—are almost invariably "caused" by factors that cannot be changed easily or at all. This is because human behavior ultimately derives from human volition—tastes, attitudes, values, and so on—and these aspects of volition in turn are either formed entirely by choice or the product of biological or social processes that we cannot or will not change.

It is the failure to understand this point that leads statesman and citizen alike to commit the causal fallacy—to assume that no problem is adequately addressed unless its causes are eliminated. The preamble to the UNESCO charter illustrates it: "Since wars begin in the minds of men it is in the minds of men that the defenses of peace must be constructed." The one thing we cannot easily do, if we can do it at all, is change, by plan and systematically, the minds of men. If peace can only be assured by doing what we cannot do, then we can never have peace. If we regard any crime-prevention or crime-reduction program as defective because it does not address the "root causes" of crime, then we shall commit ourselves to futile acts that frustrate the citizen while they ignore the criminal.

Sutherland and Cressey commit the fallacy, yet, being honest scholars, provide evidence in their own book that it *is* a fallacy. "At present," they write, "the greatest need in crime prevention is irrefutable facts about crime causation and sound means for transforming that knowledge into a program of action." [13] Suppose it could be shown that their own theory of crime causation is irrefutably correct (it may well be). The theory is that individuals commit crime when they are members of groups—families, peers, neighborhoods—that define criminal behavior as desirable.[14] The policy implication of this, which the authors draw explicitly, is that the local community must use the school, the church, the police, and other agencies to "modify" the personal groups in which crime is made to appear desirable. No indication is given as to how these agencies might do this and, given what the authors and other sociologists have said about the strength and persistence of family and friendship ties, it is hard to see what plan might be developed.

But we need not merely raise the theoretical difficulties. A series of delinquency-prevention programs have been mounted over the decades, many, if not most, of which were explicitly based on the strategy of altering primary group influences on delinquents. On the basis of careful, external evaluation, almost none can be said to have succeeded in reducing delinquency. Sutherland and Cressey describe one of the most ambitious of these, the Cambridge-Somerville Youth Study in the late 1930s. The differences in crime between those youth who were given special services (counseling, special educational programs, guidance, health assistance, camping trips) and a matched control group were insignificant: " 'the treatment' had little effect." [15]

Perhaps a better program would have better results, though it is striking, given the analysis presented so far, that for some a "better" youth project is one that goes beyond merely providing concentrated social welfare services because these services do not address the "real" causes of crime. McCord and McCord, for example, draw the lesson from the Cambridge-Somerville study that the true causes of delinquency are found in the "absence of parental affection" coupled with family conflict, inconsistent discipline, and rebellious parents. [16] They are quite possibly correct; indeed, if I may speak on the basis of my own wholly unscientific observation, I am quite confident they are correct. But what of it? What agency do we create, what budget do we allocate, that will supply the missing "parental affection" and restore to the child consistent discipline supported by a stable and loving family? When it comes to the details of their own proposals, they speak of "milieu therapy" in which the child is removed from his family and placed in a secure and permissive therapeutic environment of the sort developed by Dr. Bruno Bettelheim for autistic children. Conceding that such a program is frightfully expensive, they urge that we attempt to reach fewer children than under conventional programs, and presumably keep each child for a relatively long period. That parents, children, taxpayers, or courts might object to all this is not considered. [17]

Attempts to explain the causes of crime not only lead inevitably into the realm of the subjective and the familial, where both the efficacy and propriety of policy are most in doubt, they also lead one to a preference for the rehabilitative (or reformation) theory of corrections over the deterrence or incapacitation theories. Sutherland and Cressey recognize this: "On a formal level it may be observed that attempts to explain criminal behavior have greatly abetted at least the official use of the treatment reaction." [18] One may deter a criminal by increasing the costs or reducing the benefits of crime, but that strategy does not deal with the "causes" of criminality, and hence does not go to the "root" of the problem. Stated another way, if causal theories explain why a criminal acts as he does, they also explain why he *must* act as he does, and therefore they make any reliance on deterrence seem futile or irrelevant. Yet when Sutherland and Cressey come to consider the consequences of treating criminals in order to reform them, as opposed to punishing in order to deter them, they forthrightly admit that "there is no available proof" that treatment increased or decreased crime,[19] and that "the methods of reformation . . . have not been notably successful in reducing crime rates." [20] Careful reviews of the major efforts to rehabilitate criminals amply support this judgment.[21]

Policy analysis, as opposed to causal analysis, begins with a very different perspective. It asks not what is the "cause" of a problem, but what is the condition one wants to bring into being, what measure do we have that will tell us when that condition exists, and what policy tools does a government (in our case, a democratic and libertarian government) possess that might, when applied, produce at reasonable cost a desired alteration in the present condition or progress toward the desired condition? In this case, the desired condition is a reduction in specified forms of crime. The government has at its disposal certain—rather few, in fact—policy instruments: It can redistribute money, create (or stimulate the creation of) jobs, hire persons who offer advice, hire persons who practice surveillance and detection, build detention facilities, illuminate public streets, alter (within a range) the price of drugs and alcohol, require citizens to install alarm systems, and so on. It can, in short, manage to a degree money, prices, and technology, and it can hire people who can provide either simple (e.g., custodial) or complex (e.g., counseling) services. These tools, if employed, can affect the risks of crime, the benefits of noncriminal occupations, the accessibility of things worth stealing, and the mental state of criminals or would-be criminals. A policy analyst would ask what feasible changes in which of these instruments would, at what cost (monetary and nonmonetary), produce how much of a change in the rate of a given crime. He would suspect, from his experience in education and social services, that changing the mental state of citizens is very difficult, quite costly, hard to manage organizationally, and liable to produce many unanticipated side effects. He would then entertain as a working hypothesis that, given what he has to work with, he may gain more by altering risks, benefits, alternatives, and accessibility. He would not be sure of this, however, and would want to analyze carefully how these factors are related to existing differences in crime by state or city, and then try some experimental alterations in these factors before committing himself to them wholesale.

There is nothing that requires criminologists, as that profession is currently defined, to be policy analysts. Searching for the causes of crime is an intellectually worthy and serious undertaking, though one pursued so far in ways that are often long on theory and short on facts. I only make the point that a commitment to causal analysis, especially one that regards social processes as crucial, will rarely lead to discovering the grounds for policy choices, and such grounds as are discovered (e.g., taking children away from their parents) will raise grave ethical and political issues. Furthermore, searching for the social causes of crime will direct attention away from policy-relevant ways of explaining differences in crime rates. It was not until 1966, fifty years after criminology began as a discipline in this country and after seven editions of the leading text on crime had appeared, that there began to be a serious and sustained inquiry into the consequences for crime rates of differences in the certainty and severity of penalties.[22] Now, to an increasing extent, that inquiry is being furthered by economists rather than sociologists. This is in part because economists are by and large not interested in causality in any fundamental sense—they do not care, for example, why people buy automobiles, only that they buy fewer as the cost rises.

That criminologists gave little serious empirical attention until recently to the deterrence and accessibility aspects of crime is unfortunate; that some of them, on virtually no evidence, asserted that deterrence (usually described as "punishment") is of no value is inexcusable. Walter Reckless, for example, in the 1967 edition of his text on crime, states flatly that punishment "does not . . . prevent crime," though he adduces no systematic evidence to warrant such a conclusion.[23] Tittle and Logan provide other examples of this unsupported policy view in their survey of the more recent literature on deterrence, a survey that concludes by observing that "almost all research since 1960 supports the view that negative sanctions are significant variables in the explanation of conformity and deviance. . . . Sanctions apparently have some deterrent effect under some circumstances." [24] Whether additional research will support this tentative conclusion remains to be seen; what is clear is that modern criminology, as an intellectual enterprise, did not until very recently give serious empirical attention to the question.

In sum, the criminologist, concerned with causal explanations and part of a discipline—sociology—that assumes that social processes determine behavior, has operated largely within an intellectual framework that makes it difficult or impossible to develop reasonable policy alternatives, and has cast doubt, by assumption more than by argument or evidence, on the efficacy of those policy tools, necessarily dealing with objective rather than subjective conditions, which society might use to alter crime rates. A serious policy-oriented analysis of crime, by contrast, would place heavy emphasis on manipulation of objective conditions, not necessarily because of a belief that the "causes of crime" are thereby being eradicated, but because behavior is easier to change than attitudes, and because the only instruments society has by which to alter behavior in the short run require it to assume that people act in response to the costs and benefits of alternative courses of action. The criminologist assumes, probably rightly, that the causes of crime are determined by attitudes that in turn are socially derived, if not determined; the policy analyst is led to assume that the criminal acts *as if* crime were the product of a free choice among competing opportunities and constraints. The radical individualism of Bentham and Beccaria may be scientifically questionable but prudentially necessary.

A major apparent exception to the general perspective of criminologists is the work of Cloward and Ohlin. Writing in 1960, they developed an influential theory of delinquency in big cities. A delinquent gang (or "subculture"—the terms are used, for reasons not made clear, interchangeably) arises in response to the conflict that exists between socially approved goals (primarily monetary success) and socially approved means to realize those goals. Certain youth, notably lower-class ones, desire conventional ends but discover that there are no legitimate means to attain them; being unable (unwilling?) to revise these expectations downward, they experience frustration, and this may lead them to explore illegitimate ("nonconforming") alternatives.[25] Some lower-class youth may aspire to middle-class values ("money and morality," as the authors put it), while others may aspire only for success in lower-class terms (money alone).[26] The barriers to realizing those aspirations are found in part in cultural constraints derived from the immigrant experience (southern Italians and Sicilians, for example, allegedly do not value schooling highly), but in larger part in structural difficulties, chiefly the fact that education is costly in money outlays and foregone earnings.

In its brief form, the theory of Cloward and Ohlin would seem to be in sharp contrast to the general sociological perspective. Delinquency may be learned from peers, but it is learned because of the gap between aspirations and opportunities, and opportunities in turn are objective conditions determined by government and the social system. Education, they claim, is the chief source of opportunity. One expects Cloward and Ohlin to end their book with a call for cheaper, more readily available educational programs. But they do not. Indeed, less than one page is devoted to policy proposals, amounting essentially to one suggestion: "The major effort of those who wish to eliminate delinquency should be directed to the reorganization of slum communities." [27] No explanation is offered of what "slum reorganization" might be, except for several pages that decry the presence of "slum disorganization." Their analysis leads the reader toward the material desires of life (indeed, that is all the lower classes are supposed to value), but stops short of telling us how those material desires are realized. Their theory states that "each individual occupies a position in both legitimate and illegitimate opportunity structures" (they rightly note that this is a "new way" of viewing the problem), but they do not speak of the costs and benefits of illegitimate as opposed to legitimate opportunities.[28] Instead, the individual who is confronted with a choice among kinds of opportunities does not *choose*, he "learns deviant values" from the "social structure of the slum." [29] When the authors come to speak of policy, they have little to say about what determines the choice of illegitimate opportunities (nobody has chosen anything, he has only "learned" or "assimilated"), and thus they have no theoretical grounds for suggesting that the value of legitimate opportunities should be increased (e.g., better-paying jobs for slum youth), or that the benefits of illegitimate ones be decreased (e.g., more certain penalties for crime), or that "opportunities" for goal gratification be replaced by direct goal gratification (e.g., redistributing income). They can only write of those structures or groupings that affect learning and values, and this requires an (unexplained) "social reorganization."

The Perspective Applied

EXPLAINING human behavior is a worthwhile endeavor; indeed, for intellectuals it is among the most worthwhile. Those who search for such explanations need not justify their activity by its social utility or its policy implications. Unfortunately, neither intellectuals nor policy makers always understand this. If the government becomes alarmed about crime, it assumes that those who have studied it most deeply can contribute most fully to its solution. Criminologists have rarely sought to show statesmen the error of this assumption. Much of their writing is "practical," much of their time is "applied." To a degree, of course, criminological knowledge may assist criminologists' actions; careful study and conscientious learning can help one avoid obvious errors, attack popular myths, and devise inventive proposals. But it is also likely that the most profound understanding may impede or even distort, rather than facilitate, choice, because much of this knowledge is of what is immutable and necessary, not what is variable or contingent.

In the mid-1960s, when the federal government turned toward social scientists for help in understanding and dealing with crime, there was not in being a body of tested or even well-accepted theories as to how crime might be prevented or criminals reformed, nor was there much agreement on the "causes" of crime except that they were *social*, not psychological, biological, or individualistic. Indeed, there was not much agreement that crime was a major and growing problem—scholars noted the apparent increase in crime rates, but (properly) criticized the statistical and empirical weaknesses in these published rates. While these weaknesses did not always lead critics to conclude that crime was in fact not increasing, some scholars did draw that conclusion tentatively, and their criticisms encouraged others to draw it conclusively.

Nor were scholars very foresighted. Having established beyond doubt that crime rates are strongly related to age differences, few scholars (*none* that I can recall) noted the ominous consequences for crime of the coming-of-age in the 1960s of the postwar "baby boom." Similarly, while some scholars had shown by cross-sectional studies that the proportion of a city's population that was nonwhite was powerfully correlated with assaultive crimes, few, to my knowledge, drew the obvious implication that, unless this correlation was spurious, the continued in-migration of blacks to large cities would inflate crime rates. Once the various national commissions were underway, however, scholars associated with them (notably the group associated with the Task Force on the Assessment of Crime, under the direction of Lloyd Ohlin) began to work vigorously on these issues, and produced a number of reports that showed vividly the impact of demographic changes on crime rates.

The major intellectual difficulty governing the relationship of social scientists to policy makers with respect to crime was not the presence or absence of foresight, however, but rather the problem of how to arrive at policy proposals in the absence of scientific knowledge that would support them. The crime commission did not develop new knowledge as to crime prevention or control; as Professor Ohlin later described it, existing "social science concepts, theories and general perspectives were probably of greater utility to the staff and the Commission in forming the final recommendations than the inputs from new knowledge development efforts." [30] What were these "concepts, theories and general perspectives"? One, cited by Ohlin, consisted of "grave doubts" about the effectiveness of the criminal justice system and of rehabilitation and treatment programs. From this, Ohlin and his colleagues drew the conclusion that "the criminal justice system should be used only as a last resort in the control of undesirable conduct." From that inference, in turn, the commission adopted the view that offenders should be "diverted" from the system, and recommended a broad policy of "de-prisonization." [31]

There are no doubt ample grounds, by reason of humanity, why one would find fault with prisons, but at the time of the commission's work there were scarcely any well-established *scientific* grounds. That "treatment" had failed seemed clear, but "non-treatment" had failed just as clearly: persons on probation may be no more likely to recidivate than those in prison, but neither are they much less likely. As for deterrence, there was, when the commission deliberated and Professor Ohlin advised, virtually *no* scientific material on whether prison did or did not deter. But the commission scarcely dealt with the deterrence or incapacitation functions of prison.

In short, criminology could not form the basis for much policy advice to the commission, but that did not prevent criminologists from advising. Professor Ohlin is entirely honest about this: "The relevant social science literature was descriptive and analytical. There were relatively few experimental or controlled studies of the effectiveness of particular programs or policies. . . . Sociologists serving as consultants to the Commission proved reluctant to draw out . . . action recommendations. . . . When they did try to do this, the recommendations were often *more influenced by personal ideological convictions than by appropriately organized facts and theories* [italics added]. . . ." [32]

What were these ideologies? After an earlier version of this chapter appeared in print, one criminologist, Robert Martinson, wrote in response that his colleagues had become "advocates and spokesmen for the treatment interest and the treatment ideology, and did everything in their power to ridicule the very idea of deterrence." [33] Since he knows his professional associates better than I, there is no reason for me to reject his conclusions. Surely their role on public commissions tends to confirm it. But there is also a good deal of criminological literature that has little policy value, not because it is ideologically pro-treatment (much is in fact quite skeptical of treatment), but because it derives from an intellectual paradigm that draws attention to those features of social life least accessible to policy intervention.

Social scientists did not carry the day on the commission

(they could not, for example, get their view on marijuana accepted), but the effect of their advice, based on personal belief rather than scholarly knowledge, was clear. Working with sympathetic commission members in small task forces, the advisers stimulated and participated in a "process that led to far more liberal recommendations by the Commission than one would have thought possible at the outset given the conservative cast of its membership." [34]

There is nothing wrong with social scientists trying to persuade others of their policy beliefs, just as there is nothing wrong with conservative commission members trying to persuade sociologists of their beliefs. There *is* something wrong with a process of persuasion colored by the belief that one party to the process is an "expert" whose views are entitled to special consideration because of their evidentiary quality. There is no way of knowing to what extent commission members believed what the sociologists were saying was true, as opposed to merely plausible or interesting. But based on my own experience in advising national commissions, including the crime commission, I am confident that few social scientists made careful distinctions, when the chips were down, between what they knew as scholars and what they believed as citizens, or even spent much time discussing the complex relationships between knowledge and belief. I certainly did not, and I do not recall others doing so.

Having alluded to my own role as a policy adviser, let me amplify on that experience to reenforce, by self-criticism, the point I am making. I was not in 1966 a criminologist, nor am I now. I came to crime, if I may put it that way, as a consequence of my study of police administration and its political context, and found myself labeled an "expert" on crime because of that interest, and perhaps also because of the desire of governmental consumers of "expertise" to inflate, by wishful thinking, the supply of such persons to equal the demand for their services.

Once I found myself in the crime business, I found that my

ideas on the subject—apart from those formed by my empirical research on policing—were inevitably influenced by the currents of academic opinion about me. The effect of these currents is not to persuade one of what is important, but to persuade one of what is interesting. In my case, I did not absorb from criminological writings a set of policy conclusions about whether criminals can be deterred or rehabilitated, but I did absorb a set of "interesting facts" about crime: for example, crimes are age-specific, victims contribute to their victimization in most assaultive crimes, and published crime rates are unreliable. All of these things were (and are) true, but of course they are not directly related to the policy question of what is to be done about crime.

These things were thought important by social scientists with whom I spoke because they were not widely known; they constituted, so to speak, the "unconventional wisdom." Social scientists generally, and practitioners of the "softer" social sciences in particular, are in their day-to-day work preoccupied with things they know that others do not, rather than (as their critics sometimes allege) with their cherished ideologies or favorite policy nostrums. This preoccupation arises in part out of the natural pleasures of discovery and in part out of the professional rewards that accrue to originality and critical skills and the professional penalties that are imposed on naïveté and conventionality. It was only gradually, as I became involved in various advisory roles, that I realized that what is interesting is not necessarily useful.

In short, I did not, any more than Professor Ohlin, have in 1966–1968 empirically supported policy advice to offer statesmen dealing with crime. What I then realized, as did Professor Ohlin, was that many of those seated about me, urging in the strongest tones various "solutions" to crime, were speaking out of ideology, not scholarship. Only later did I realize that criminologists and perhaps all sociologists, are part of an intellectual tradition that does not contain built-in checks against the premature conversion of opinion into policy, because the focal concerns of that tradition are with those aspects of society that are, to a great extent, beyond the reach of policy and even beyond the reach of science. Those matters that are within the reach of policy have been, at least for many criminologists, defined as uninteresting because they were superficial, "symptomatic," or not of "causal" significance. Sociology, for all its claims to understand structure, is at heart a profoundly subjectivist discipline. When those who practice it are brought forward and asked for advice, they will say either (if conservative) that nothing is possible, or (if liberal) that everything is possible. That most sociologists are liberals explains why the latter reaction is more common, even though the presuppositions of their own discipline would more naturally lead to the former.

Chapter 4

Politicians

O<small>NE WOULD</small> suppose that politicians, in their competitive struggle for votes, would have seized upon the issue of crime almost as soon as the crime rates had started up, and, in seizing it, would have devoted their energies to outbidding each other in ways to give immediate and visible protection to its victims. Statesmen might take a longer, or at least less emotional, view of the problem; criminologists might continue their efforts to clarify its causes; but surely politicians would be quick to respond to—perhaps even to exploit—rising popular fears of crime.

To some degree they did. In the 1964 presidential campaign, Barry Goldwater attacked the incumbent administration for its inattention to "crime in the streets." Here and there—Minneapolis is an example—a "law-and-order" candidate was elected mayor. In the mid-1960s, however, much of the rhetoric about law and order was directed not at ordinary predatory crime, but at the black riots in the cities. It was being voiced by politicians who represented not the victims of the riots or even the victims of common crime, but those more affluent citizens who were symbolically outraged at but not personally harmed by deviant behavior. Political leaders who represented the ordinary victims of ordinary crime, black and white, had rather little to say about the subject and thus, almost by default, crime came to be seen as a "conservative" issue of largely symbolic significance.

By the time of the 1970 congressional elections, this was beginning to change. President Nixon and Vice-President Agnew in that campaign tried to attack the Democrats on crime and other aspects of what was later to be called the "social issue," but their strategy had little apparent success and may in fact have backfired. By this time Democratic candidates had begun to develop a strong anticrime posture of their own, thereby neutralizing the Republican advantage in this area and forcing the campaign toward conventional issues of incumbency, taxes, and unemployment. In short, the Democrats moved back to the political center. By the time of the 1972 presidential campaign, crime was scarcely a partisan issue at all.

But why had the Democrats deserted the political center on this issue in the first place? That they did for much of the 1960s is beyond question. In May 1965 the Gallup Poll reported that for the first time "crime" (along with education) was viewed by Americans as the most important problem facing the nation. More careful surveys done over the next two years, some under the sponsorship of the president's crime commission, confirmed and amplified this finding. At about that time I happened to be supervising the survey described in Chapter 1 and noted the striking fact that when asked what was the biggest problem facing large cities, black respondents were more likely to mention crime and juvenile delinquency than any other issue. Most whites agreed with them, though Italians and Poles put "the Negro problem" slightly ahead of lawlessness. It struck me that "crime in the streets" could not be simply a codeword for antiblack feeling if blacks themselves were voicing it.

In the months leading up to the Democratic National Convention in 1968—specifically in February, May, and August—Gallup continued to report crime as the most important issue, now accompanied by Vietnam and the high cost of living. Not only was the crime issue important to millions of voters, most of the voters who were the victims of street crime were Democrats—blacks, poor whites living in big cities, and upper-middle-class Jewish professionals living in midtown Manhattan. By contrast, Orange County suburbanites who complained a lot about crime rarely experienced it and would vote Republican anyway. Furthermore, crime—unlike Vietnam and inflation—was not an issue for which the Democrats had to explain away their part in causing it. The president may have sent troops to Vietnam, but he had not sent muggers to East 67th Street; he may have overheated the economy, but he had not opened the prison gates. One would naturally suppose that much would be made of the crime issue at the convention.

One's natural guess would have been wrong. To be sure, the keynote speaker deplored crime and the platform called for implementing the crime commission recommendations. More revealing was the conduct of what some might have thought to be the two major interest groups speaking for the problems of urban America—the AFL–CIO, representing labor, and the Urban Coalition, attempting (in vain) to represent everybody else. Both organizations presented elaborate statements to the platform committee. Crime was mentioned only in passing, and though many proposals were made on all other aspects of urban life, none was made in the area of criminal justice. The attorney general of the United States, Ramsey Clark, was quoted as saying, no doubt in an unguarded moment, that he did not think the United States was having a crime wave at all.

In the actual campaigning, individual candidates began to sense the importance of this and related issues. Robert Kennedy, speaking in the closing days of the Indiana primary, had given major emphasis to his opposition to crime and his desire to find a way to put welfare recipients to work. Hubert Humphrey, after his nomination, issued a lengthy statement on what was now rechristened "order and justice." Eugene McCarthy, as far as anyone can tell, never sensed the issue at all.

After Humphrey's defeat, the center of activity—if not of votes—within the Democratic National Committee and its allied policy groups became expressive of the "New Politics" and the determination of those gifted at it to move the Democratic party to the left. It is, of course, normal for the party out of power to acquire as spokesmen those at the ideological extreme; any number can play the game of being against the incumbent administration, and those most willing to play without remuneration are usually those ideologically most highly committed.

Meanwhile, those who aspired to hold office were paying a heavy price for being caught on the wrong side of a major issue. An attractive black candidate could not beat an undistinguished Los Angeles mayor; in losing, Thomas Bradley could not manage to win the large majorities usually available to liberals in the Jewish precincts. A law-and-order mayor won in Minneapolis with almost no credentials but his position on crime. Another law-and-order candidate was beaten in Detroit, but only, it would appear, because she had the misfortune to run against a Polish ex-sheriff (who turned out to be a "moderate" on the police issue). And John Lindsay—the liberal mayor of the most liberal city in the nation—"won" reelection only because it was a three-man race. As Scammon and Wattenberg later put it: What kind of would-be national Democratic politician is it who can carry, in his own city, only a quarter of the votes of the white working class and less than half the votes of the Jews? [1]

A major problem facing anyone seeking to give an account of party politics in the 1960s is why a party with which a majority of the voters identify, confronting an issue of great practical importance to its own rank and file and of great symbolic importance to everyone else, and in a position to take the initiative rather than defend a record, chose to display itself in a manner leading millions of its own followers to think of it as wrong.

The explanation is to be found in the fact that while the forces impelling the major parties to move toward the center at the time of a national presidential election are usually quite strong, the forces impelling them to move away from the center between those elections have become in recent years almost equally strong. As long as the chief prize of politics is the presidency, and as long as there are for all practical purposes only two contenders for that prize, finding and moving toward the center is the inevitable strategy of each contender. But during the three-and-a-half years when no presidential contest is underway, the parties must decide to which of many competing internal pressures they will respond. Increasingly, those internal pressures—in both parties, but especially the Democratic—led key party figures to occupy positions far from the center.

Chief among these internal forces are those exerted by persons whose volunteer contributions to the party are deemed essential and whose esteem is deemed worth winning. For the Democrats, these persons include activist professors whose advice—and more important, whose blessing—is valued; friendly syndicated columnists and key editors and reporters in the "national" press (the *New York Times*, the *Washington Post*, *Newsweek*, and so on) from whom the assurance of sympathetic treatment must be won; well-to-do individuals, mostly in New York (and some in Los Angeles), who are prepared to give substantial sums even to unlikely, high-risk candidates if they feel strongly enough about "the issues"; and volunteer workers available on an ad hoc basis for individual campaign organizations when and if they find those individuals attractive.

Some may see in this nothing more than a rehash of familiar charges about the "Eastern liberal establishment" that "dictates" policies and "selects" candidates. But this simplistic view is inadequate, both in suggesting a level of agreement on issues that does not exist and in failing to explain why so few people can wield so much influence over supposedly canny professional politicians. There is in fact nothing conspiratorial about the sources of liberalism in the Democratic party, just as there is nothing spooky or pathological about the sources (and influence) of Goldwater-Reagan conservatism in the Republican.

Between elections "the party" hardly exists except as a label. Between elections, the political process, especially among those not in national office, consists in great measure of engaging in a partly competitive, partly cooperative struggle to marshal or husband valued political resources—visibility, reputation, allies, money, followers. The net effect of this struggle at any point in time is measured in terms of the "standing" of various political figures, that standing being a composite of "soundness," "style," and "appeal." Increasingly, the standing is judged in terms of ideas, and in this way ideas tend to have consequences. Ideas in American politics usually do not affect the course of events because masses of people are persuaded of them (though that sometimes happens—an "idea whose time has come"), but because to a great extent the standing of individual politicians has been determined in light of the ideas (as well as style and appeal) valued by the attentive audience of those politicians. The good reputation of the politicians, in turn, is communicated to the general citizenry, not so much in terms of statements that say "Senator Jones is a good man because of his position on poverty," but rather in such forms as "Senator Jones is a good man because he has a position on poverty," or better yet, "Senator Jones cares" or is "concerned." Caring—empathy—is the vulgar expression of ideology, where ideology exists. Sometimes empathy is an expression of nothing at all.

The influence of this attentive audience increased during the 1960s in both political parties, but particularly in the Democratic. And the attentive Democratic audience is liberal, made up of volunteers and part-time public servants with discretionary money to spend, personal style to display, campaign skills to use, "interesting ideas" to propound, and influence in the mass media to wield. The importance of the members of the liberal audience has grown as the power and cohesiveness of the political party at the local level declined; as the bright young millionaires created by the boom of the 1960s became interested in applying their social conscience to politics; as television acquired a power to bless or curse formerly reserved to archbishops; as organized labor came to be scorned for its "middle-class values" (though courted for its working-class money); and as key posts in city halls, federal agencies, and even the White House were filled with brilliant young men fresh out of law school or sometimes even fresher out of college. To a substantial degree, at least on the East Coast, Democratic politics when the party is out of power occurs within this group and the several communications nets linking it.

To some extent a comparable process was underway in the Republican party. The nomination of Goldwater was a triumph of the volunteer spirit among Republicans and exceedingly pleasing to those conservative intellectuals and fund givers who had long chafed under the center-seeking tendencies of the party, a process they liked to call "me-too-ism." But the difference between what happened in 1964 to the Republicans and what happened in 1965–1970 to the Democrats is that the rise of amateur politics among the Republicans was led and symbolized by one man who was an active candidate; the high-water mark of conservative ideology was his nomination and the low-water mark his defeat. With Goldwater's loss, those identified with him were at a profound disadvantage in the party; many, indeed, became more interested in Governor Reagan in California. But amateur politics in the Democratic party was not identified with or led by a single candidate; to a considerable degree the movement took strength from its opposition to the party's leader, President Johnson. To the extent that the liberal audience identified with any political figures, none of those it identified with until 1972 ever lost a national election: McCarthy could not win the nomination, Robert Kennedy was murdered, George McGovern was not a serious contender before 1972, and Ramsey Clark did not enter electoral politics until 1974.

The rise in importance of the liberal audience was not checked by electoral realities until 1972. The rise itself, however, cannot be explained merely in terms of a change in the distribution of political resources. To be sure, the television medium is more powerful than before, idea men are in demand, and fund givers for high-risk candidates are valued. But all this might not have produced the extraordinary shift in the Demo-

cratic party's center of gravity had it not been for other processes
that were also at work. The most significant of these changes
was the loss of political and moral authority by the old sources
of party leadership. As late as 1960 Mayor Richard Daley of
Chicago was held in high esteem by many liberals, not simply
because he was an effective mayor but because he had helped
nominate Adlai Stevenson in 1956 and John F. Kennedy in
1960. Kennedy became President of the United States because
old-line party bosses gave him the nomination and helped give
him the election (anyone who doubts the latter statement need
only recall the long delay in the Chicago returns in that November of 1960 when the outcome depended almost entirely on
the Illinois electoral votes).

The voters at large were increasingly suspicious of party
"bosses," finding men who practiced politics out of self-interest
or in ways that catered to the particular self-interest of others
distasteful. The chic of the Kennedy administration did not
cause this change, but it helped it along—Daley might get a few
laughs welcoming Queen Elizabeth to Chicago, but no one
could imagine inviting him to the White House to hear Pablo
Casals. Thus, long before Daley's police hit anybody in Grant
Park, it seemed to many that to govern the nation in the 1960s
it was more important to understand "fiscal drag" and "second-
strike capability" and "counterinsurgency warfare" (or at least be
able to mention them knowingly; very few really understood
those phrases) than it was to tend to what party leaders were saying. In the first place they seemed to be saying irrelevant or out-
of-date things; second, they didn't say them very grammatically;
third, "everybody knew" their days were numbered; fourth, the
federal government, through various antipoverty programs, was
going to build a rival and more enduring political structure in
the big cities; fifth, the federal government was going to "by-
pass" the states (and thus state party structures) and deal directly
with urban problems; and sixth, and perhaps most important,
the party bosses were not very good when it came to dealing
with blacks.

And they weren't. A party is an aggregation of interests; a party leader is a man who maintains the aggregation. Men who build coalitions or maintain aggregations tend not to emphasize larger principles, especially those that will divide the coalition. Men who are good horse traders rarely clarify or advance the rule of law except as it applies to horses. Reasons one through five in the preceding paragraph might explain the decline in the political authority of party leaders; the sixth reason explains their decline in moral authority.

But where would new party leadership of matters of race come from? And what would it do? The central problem, apparent only in retrospect, was that if the party leaders seemed to lack the moral authority to deal with the black question, the liberal audience—a group rooted in the upper middle class— lacked the knowledge. There were three sources of knowledge about blacks—census data, militant black spokesmen, and slum romanticism. A few first-hand studies existed, but not many. The economists, but few others, paid great attention to the census data. Militant blacks and slum romantics quickly found they could agree on rather little—blacks were beginning to object to whites who thought they "understood the Negro"—but on one principle they could agree: there was no "Negro problem," there was only a "white problem." It was not until the Kerner commission that this doctrine received the imprimatur of a presidential agency, but it was the operating doctrine long before it was set in type by the Government Printing Office.

To a great extent, this doctrine was an advance. It repudiated Southern racist notions of white supremacy; it forced on one's consciousness the realization that race was a national responsibility; and it directed attention toward the need for a change in white attitudes and white practices without waiting for blacks to be "ready" for the change. The doctrine also conferred some political advantages in intraparty struggle; it was an explicit rejection of the old-line party leaders' private view that blacks were like any other ethnic group, except with less gumption, and should be treated accordingly.

But there were costs to this doctrine. One, relevant to the argument here, is that it became impossible to construct a political strategy that rested on finding what problems blacks and whites had in common. Politics, under the "white racism" doctrine, became a zero-sum game—anything blacks win, whites must lose, and vice versa. There are some problems like that, but most are not. Crime is one of the former.

The fact that blacks commit a disproportionate share of certain crimes (not by any means of all crimes) led those who spoke for or about blacks in the 1960s either to deny the fact ("We all know crime statistics are inaccurate"), to explain it as the result of a discriminatory police system ("They pick on blacks"), or to argue that blacks are driven to it by poverty and segregation ("They can't get a job legally so they must earn money illegally"). There is some truth in all of these points, but only some; taken as a full account of the matter they are seriously inadequate. A different perspective on crime, one easily available to a person of reasonable sense who lived in the inner city, was that no matter who was committing crimes, the victims were disproportionately blacks, police protection was inadequate, and more efficient (and fairer) deterrence and apprehension systems were immediate needs. Here, as with many social problems, it is necessary to deal with symptoms before one can deal with causes.

The war in Southeast Asia completed the discrediting of established leaders within the party. The left wing of the party was calling on the United States to leave Vietnam at a time when the more conventional, in-and-out-of-government members of the liberal audience were merely calling for an end of the bombing of North Vietnam. After the Cambodian excursion, the conventional liberals decided that they, too, wanted out. The left then seemed to have been correct all along, and consequently at a considerable advantage when it came to asserting moral authority.

Under these circumstances, for a Democrat to have voiced a serious concern for crime (and not merely for those social problems, such as poverty, which may be related to crime) would have placed him at a hopeless moral disadvantage. He would be appearing to favor the police over the poor, Mayor Daley over college youth, repression over freedom, George Wallace over George McGovern. It would have taken considerable skill and courage to say in response that there was a position on crime that did not require one to endorse Mayor Daley or Governor Wallace, or to "unleash" the police and "handcuff" the courts.

Such a position existed, however. Its general points would have been about as follows: First, the rise in the rate of predatory crime—especially "street crime"—was real and dramatic and neither a statistical artifact nor an FBI public relations stunt; second, blacks and whites alike were the victims of crime (blacks more than whites), and thus blacks and whites alike had a common interest in its control; third, the increase came concurrently with a general rise in the standard of living and thus could not be explained by worsening social conditions; fourth, though continued improvements in prosperity and in ending discrimination may ultimately be the best remedies for crime, in the short term (anything less than the next generation or two) society's efforts must be aimed at improving the criminal justice system as a mechanism for just and effective social control; fifth, any such improvements must focus as much on the criminal courts and the correctional system as on the police, because these institutions are failing to deal with persons already identified as criminal repeaters; and sixth, there must be a massive effort to cut off the flow of heroin into this country and to extend the use of chemical alternatives to heroin addiction.

To many readers today, these points will seem self-evident. For their benefit let me recount what was (and is) typically heard as the alternative position: The rise in crime is illusory or exaggerated; whites are using the crime issue as a way of expressing racist sentiments; if there is a real increase in crime, only remedying the underlying social causes with bigger expenditures on poverty programs will make any real difference; the overriding need in dealing with the criminal justice system is to make it fairer, not to make it more effective; and much so-called "crime" would be eliminated if we did not "overcriminalize" behavior by making public intoxication and the sale of marijuana illegal.

I believe each of these propositions is factually wrong or seriously misleading; other chapters offer some evidence on this score. The point being made here, however, is that those who took these latter positions had no right to be surprised when so many citizens seemed more inclined to listen to voices from the right which promised a reduction in crime if the Supreme Court could be impeached, the attorney general replaced, and the death penalty restored. I believe each of these propositions was also wrong, but I must concede their rhetorical impact—an impact made all the greater by the abdication by one party of any effective interest in the problem.

Looking back on the late 1960s, one can take comfort from the fact that, although not much was done well, rather little was done that made matters clearly worse. The political right was given almost a monopoly over the crime issue, but it was not as a result able to produce much substantive change. The Supreme Court was not impeached, no one was sent to the gallows, and the best that could be said of the new attorney general was that he had the good fortune to be in office when the crime rate in several cities briefly leveled off or went down for reasons utterly unrelated to his incumbency.

And by 1970, enough members of the liberal audience had had their typewriters stolen to make it difficult to write articles denying the existence of a crime wave. When, during the 1970 campaign, a national columnist published an article deploring the tendency of Democrats to dwell on the crime issue and urging them to "skirt or mute" it, there appeared in the same issue of the same magazine an article entitled "A Nervous New Yorker's Guide to Safety Devices," offering a careful evaluation of various gadgets for defending a Manhattan apartment against burglary.

Liberalism arose in the nineteenth century as a set of ideas opposed to despotic authority, and consisted chiefly of the rule of law, representative government, and civil liberties. To this came to be added an equally strong concern for advancing welfare and social amelioration. Both sets of ideas had essentially utilitarian justifications—society would be "better off" if government respected personal liberty and advanced social welfare. Since the advent of the New Deal, and especially since the Supreme Court began after 1936 to support welfare measures, the procedural elements of the liberal creed have steadily been lost sight of or taken for granted. McCarthyism briefly called forth their reassertion, but that is now a generation past. The growing preoccupation with social welfare, and the apparent ease with which American society seemed to hold together and the democratic process seemed to work, made many liberals almost entirely result-oriented. Programs and ideas were to be judged by the extent to which they conferred benefits on particular groups of people. It was assumed that the law would be obeyed.

This shift changed the central tendency of liberalism from commitment to certain ideas to the manifestation of concern or empathy for certain worthy others. There was little wrong and much that was generous and decent about this impulse, but it increasingly left liberals unprepared for the day when the law would no longer be obeyed and personal liberty no longer respected.

Among the happier consequences of the Watergate scandal has been a general reawakening of a concern for ensuring that political action is always subordinate to the essential laws of a free society. "Caring" about the adverse impact of unpopular views or the theft of government documents no more justifies illegal behavior than caring about the plight of the poor justifies overlooking crimes they may commit. Happily, by 1974 almost no one was saying that a man is entitled to rob a bank so long as high White House officials could get away with criminal acts, just as almost no one was saying that these officials may rifle private files and suborn perjury so long as some men get away with robbing banks. In ways that Attorney General Mitchell never intended, the Republicans restored the good name of prisons.

PART
III
DEALING WITH CRIME

Chapter 5

The Police
and Crime

HE average citizen thinks of the police as an organization primarily concerned with preventing crime and catching criminals. When crime increases or criminals go uncaught, the conventional public response is to demand more or better policemen. When the crime rate goes down or a particularly heinous crime is solved, the police often get—or at least try to take—the credit.

For some time, persons who run or study police departments have recognized that this public conception is misleading. The majority of calls received by most police are for services that have little to do with crime but a great deal to do with medical emergencies, family quarrels, auto accidents, barking dogs, minor traffic violations, and so on. And those calls that do involve serious crimes, such as burglaries, robberies, and auto thefts, typically occur after the event has taken place and the trail is cold; the officer who responds can often do little more than fill out a report that will contain few if any leads for further investigation.[1] The police themselves wish it were otherwise—most patrolmen would prefer to stop a crime in progress or catch a major felon—but only infrequently do they have the chance.

The growing realization among scholars and administrators of the importance of the service provision, order maintenance function of patrolmen has led some experts to dismiss or downplay the crime control function. A police department is often thought "advanced" or "progressive" to the extent it emphasizes community service rather than crime prevention. To a degree, this is well and good: For too long, police officers were given little training and no supervision in the performance of their most frequent duties, with the result that many citizens felt poorly treated and many officers felt frustrated and unsure of their mission.

But progress along these lines does not constitute an answer to the citizen's concern with crime. He believes, with reason, that if there were no police at all there would be more crime, and therefore he supposes that if there were more police there would be less crime. When he sees a policeman on a street corner, the citizen often feels more secure and assumes that the burglar or mugger seeing the same officer will feel less secure. If a crime is committed, the citizen believes that the police should diligently look for the criminal, even if it means neglecting their community service functions. The citizen is impatient with theories that argue that crime can only be prevented by reforming prisons or ending poverty. He thinks that crime—or at least crime that affects him—will be prevented if sufficient policemen walk by his home or business often enough.

There have been some attempts to test that belief, but until recently these efforts had serious shortcomings. One of the first was carried out in 1954 by the New York City Police Department (NYPD) under the direction of Commissioner Francis W. H. Adams.[2] Beginning on September 1 of that year, the police strength assigned to the twenty-fifth precinct in Manhattan (comprising much of East Harlem) was more than doubled.

Most of the additional men were inexperienced patrolmen taken straight from the Police Academy who were assigned to foot posts, although experienced detectives and traffic, juvenile, and narcotics officers were also added to the precinct. Before the experiment, called "Operation 25," began, as many as two-thirds of the foot posts (or beats) in the area were unmanned. During the experiment, no post was left vacant, the number was increased from fifty-five to eighty-nine, and their average length was shortened.

Operation 25 lasted four months. During that time serious crimes declined and the reduction was greatest for "street crimes"—those that either occurred in public places or involved entry from the street into private places. Muggings fell from sixty-nine during the same period in 1953 to seven in the experimental part of 1954, and auto thefts dropped from seventy-eight to twenty-four. Burglaries declined as well, especially those for which the entry was made from the front of the residence or store. Murder, essentially a "private" crime, did not decline at all; indeed, it increased from six to eight cases. Felonious assault, which, like murder, frequently occurs in private places among "friends," did decline, but not nearly as much as street robberies or auto thefts.

Operation 25 was used to justify to the mayor and city council police demands for increases in manpower. The increases were forthcoming. Between 1954 and 1974, the size of the NYPD increased by 54 per cent, while the total population remained about constant. However, crime increased even more rapidly than the police.

The subsequent increase in crime despite the growth in the size of the police force does not necessarily repudiate the findings of Operation 25. After all, the composition of the population has changed substantially during the years since 1954. Furthermore, not all officers added to a police department are added to the effective street force of that department. Thus, for every hundred officers added to the force, only a few may represent net increments to street patrol.

But if later history did not disprove Operation 25, problems in its design raised questions about its significance. There was no direct measure of true crime rates, only counts of reported crimes. More important, the comparison in crime rates was made with crime the preceding year. It is possible that crime might have declined during 1954 for reasons other than the increased police presence. But most important, no effort was made to discover whether crime in surrounding precincts increased as a result of the increased police activity of Operation 25. Perhaps crime was not reduced, only displaced. Finally, police administrators, if not citizens, would want to know whether increases of police manpower short of doubling the previous number will have any effect, and whether patrolmen in cars are more or less effective than those on foot.

In the 1960s, there were some fresh efforts to answer these questions. In Great Britain, J. A. Bright of the Home Office reported on the "Beat Patrol Experiments" carried out in 1965 to discover whether the number of crimes in an urban area would be affected by the number of foot patrolmen in that area.[3] In four British cities a number of foot beats were designated as experimental areas, and over successive four-week periods the number of officers walking those beats was varied systematically between zero and four. At the end of one year, Bright and his colleagues concluded that the number of reported crimes on a beat decreased when the officers patrolling it on foot increased from zero to one, but that there were no further decreases resulting from raising the number of patrolmen to two per beat. There was some tentative evidence that a really sharp increase— say, from one to three or even four officers on a single beat— would produce still further reductions in crime, but the evidence supporting this was weak, and in any event it is not generally feasible to triple or quadruple a city's police force. In sum, Bright rejected the view that having more foot patrolmen in a neighborhood will produce a reduction in crime. Unfortunately, the beats in which the experiment was conducted were so small and the periods during which the changes were made so brief that the Home Office results can at best be regarded as tentative.

At about the same time, another project was underway in New York that sought to measure the results of having more cops on the beat. One of the objectives of this study, carried out by S. J. Press for the New York City Rand Institute, was to look closely at the possibility, overlooked in Operation 25, that reported crime rates might change for reasons having nothing to do with the additional officers on patrol.[4] To this end, Press studied two nearby precincts similar to the one (the twentieth precinct) in which, beginning in October 1966, police manpower was increased by 40 per cent, while the manpower assigned in the rest of the city remained about what it had always been.

The results, though not quite as dramatic as those claimed for Operation 25, were on the whole quite consistent with it. In the twentieth precinct, street robberies per week fell by 33 per cent, auto theft by 49 per cent, and grand larcencies "visible from the street" by 49 per cent. There were no appreciable decreases in serious crimes that occurred in private places, such as burglary and assault. Most important, these were *net* reductions in crime, over and above such changes as may have occurred in the similar precincts in which no additional policemen were deployed. Furthermore, these reductions seemed to be genuine—that is, little evidence was found that crime had simply been displaced to adjoining precincts.

Though the data from the twentieth precinct were better analyzed than had been those from the twenty-fifth precinct, the results were still inconclusive. Only changes in reported crimes, not in actual crimes, could be observed, and the reporting system itself changed early in the project, perhaps affecting the results in unknown ways. The time period was short—four months in the case of Operation 25, eight months in the twentieth precinct. Perhaps a sudden increase in police manpower will make criminals lie low or go elsewhere for a while, but then, as they become accustomed to the new situation, they resume their activities. This is often exactly what happens when better street lights are installed; crime decreases for a while but then returns to its previous level. Only rudimentary efforts were made to match socioeconomically the areas in which the police were strengthened with those in which they were not. In short, neither project was a true experiment.

Nonetheless, even discounting the results substantially to allow for these imperfections, the results in the two New York projects were sufficiently striking and consistent to warrant entertaining the belief that very large increases in police patrols may reduce "outside" or "street" crime significantly, at least for a short period of time.

Some of the limitations of the early studies were overcome in a careful analysis of subway robberies in New York City and the effect of increased assignment of police to the subway system. The proportion of crimes committed that are actually reported is probably much higher in the subway than in the city as a whole, because many victims are transit employees who must report crimes if they are to account for missing cash and tokens. And citizen victims are delivered by the subway to stops where police, dispatchers, and change-booth clerks are readily available, thus facilitating the reporting of a loss.

The two most common major crimes in subways are the robbing of passengers, an offense typically committed by young black boys of school age who, though unarmed, often use violence, and the robbing of change-booth clerks, a crime typically committed by somewhat older males, frequently narcotics users, who, though armed with guns, rarely use violence.

In the two years preceding 1965, subway felonies were increasing at an annual rate of about 50 per cent. In April of that year, Mayor Robert Wagner ordered a substantial increase in police patrols in the subways, from twelve hundred persons to over thirty-one hundred, with the objective, which was by and large met, of having a police officer on every subway train and at every station between the hours of 8 P.M. and 4 A.M.

The results of this manning schedule over an eight-year

period were later analyzed by Jan M. Chaiken, Michael W. Lawless, and Keith A. Stevenson at the New York City Rand Institute.[5] This evaluation covers the longest period of patrol work ever studied in a comparable fashion. Following the introduction of heavy police coverage in 1965, there was a short-term decline in total subway crime. Within a year or so, however, the number of subway robberies began to rise again at a rapid rate, so that by 1970 there were six times as many robberies occurring as had occurred in 1965, when the extra police were first hired.

This discouraging result in total subway robberies concealed, however, a remarkable success story. The extra police were primarily deployed during the evening. The number of subway felonies occurring per hour during the night fell in 1965 *and remained low,* while the number of felonies occurring during the day, after a brief decrease in 1965 when the publicity about more transit police was at its peak, rose more or less steadily from 1966 on.

The Rand authors concluded that, though subway crime has tended to rise year after year, the addition of uniformed officers to the trains and platforms during the evening hours has caused a substantial decline in crime at those times, and that this deterrent effect of the police has persisted for several years. The cost was high, however—about $35,000 per deterred felony. And the circumstances were quite special: the subway is an enclosed place with few exits. A would-be robber, seeing a police officer on a train or platform, will find it difficult to select a victim sufficiently removed from the officer as to eliminate the chance of being caught in the act, and to discover an escape route sufficiently convenient as to give him a good chance of getting away once a hue and cry is set up. In short, the subway patrol plan, while apparently of considerable value when it is in effect, offers few guidelines for patrolling the city streets.

In the late 1960s there was being developed a major new research technique of great potential value in studying police effectiveness. This was the "victimization survey," pioneered by the Task Force on the Assessment of Crime of President Johnson's Commission on Law Enforcement and Administration of Justice. A national survey of ten thousand households was carried out in 1966 by Philip H. Ennis and the National Opinion Research Center of the University of Chicago. Simultaneously, a survey of over five hundred persons in three precincts of Washington, D.C., was undertaken by Albert D. Biderman and the Bureau of Social Science Research, Inc.[6]

These surveys provided for the first time convincing evidence of the extent of unreported crime, a fact now widely accepted. There were, we learned, about twice as many major crimes being committed in the United States every year than appeared in official police statistics. In 1972–1973, the United States Bureau of the Census conducted even larger victimization surveys and in general confirmed the earlier finding.

The 1966 surveys, being one-shot enterprises, could not tell us anything about *changes* in true crime rates. But they offered a technique which, though quite expensive, could be applied to experiments in police patrol. By measuring victimization rates of individuals and business firms in experimental areas before and after changes in police deployment, and also in carefully matched control areas where no changes in deployment occurred, more reliable conclusions could be drawn about the extent to which various police strategies could affect crime.

In the early 1970s a few big-city police departments devised and began such experiments with funds, technical assistance, and evaluation studies provided by the Police Foundation, a private, independent foundation in Washington, D.C., created in the summer of 1970 by the Ford Foundation.

The first to be completed was done in Kansas City, Missouri, to test the effect of different levels of "preventive patrol." Preventive patrol, for long the fundamental assumption of police deployment, means having officers walk or drive through their beats whenever they are not answering a specific call for service or assistance. By their continuous, moving presence, so the theory goes, crime will be prevented because would-be criminals will be aware of and deterred by the police presence. Furthermore, this patrolling may enable the officer to witness a crime in progress or to discover and stop fugitives, suspicious persons, and stolen cars.

Officers in Kansas City designed an experiment to test these assumptions. In the southern part of the city, fifteen police beats were sorted into five groups of three matched beats each. Each group was made up of beats that were as similar as possible in population characteristics (income, ethnicity, transiency, and so on), reported crime levels, and calls for police services. Within each group, three different patrol strategies were used for a one-year period. One beat (chosen at random) was patrolled in the customary fashion by a single patrol car that cruised the streets whenever it was not answering calls. These were the "control" beats. A second beat in each group had a greatly increased level of preventive patrol—cars were visible cruising these streets two to three times more frequently than in the control areas. This strategy was called "proactive patrol." In the third beat in each group, preventive patrol was eliminated altogether—a police car would enter the area only in answer to a specific request for service. When that run was completed, the car would either return to the periphery of the beat or cruise streets outside it. This was called "reactive patrol." Before and after the experiment, individuals and businessmen were interviewed to learn whether they had been the victims of crime, what they thought of the quality of police service, and to what extent they were fearful of crime.

The results analyzed by George L. Kelling and others were startling. After a year, no substantial differences among the three areas were observed in criminal activity, amount of reported crime, rate of victimization as revealed in the follow-up survey, level of citizen fear, or degree of citizen satisfaction with the police. For all practical purposes, the changes in the level of preventive patrol made no difference at all.

For reasons that are still hard to understand, citizen respect for the police increased somewhat in the control beats, where nothing was changed, and did not increase at all (indeed, declined slightly) on the proactive beats, where more police became available. And strangest of all, perhaps, the citizen living on the proactive beats felt more apprehensive than those living on others about the likelihood of being robbed or raped.

It is easy to misinterpret these results, and so it is important to state what was *not* found. The experiment does *not* show that the police make no difference and it does *not* show that adding more police is useless in controlling crime. All it shows is that changes in the amount of random preventive patrol in marked cars does not, by itself, seem to affect, over one year's time in Kansas City, how much crime occurs or how safe citizens feel. Very different results may have been obtained if important changes were made in *how* the police were used—for example, by having them patrol in unmarked cars, by having them walk beats out of uniform, by directing them to place under continuing surveillance frequently victimized homes or stores, or by assigning them to do more thorough follow-up investigations of crimes. Studies are underway that may shed some light on a few of these alternatives.

Even so, the Kansas City results offer an important opportunity for police administrators and public officials. If true generally and not just in one city, then these findings mean that there is no compelling reason to tie up large numbers of uniformed officers in the monotonous and apparently unproductive task of driving through the streets waiting for something to happen. By cutting back on preventive patrol, a substantial amount of manpower—in Kansas City, perhaps as much as one-third of all patrol man-hours—could be made available for other tasks, such as investigation, surveillance, or community service.

The key question, therefore, is whether other ways of using patrolmen will be more effective in terms of crime control or citizen satisfaction. Two kinds of patrol strategies have been designed to replace preventive patrol. One is the "community service" approach. It is based on the assumption that if officers are encouraged to become familiar with the neighborhoods in which they work and to take larger responsibilities for following through on citizen requests for assistance as well as on complaints of crime, they will win the confidence of those whom they are to protect and thereby elicit more cooperative assistance from the public and better intelligence about criminal activities. The other is the "crime attack" model which, while not logically incompatible with the former, is based on the assumption that the best use of patrolmen is to place them as close as possible, not to the citizens, but to the scene of a potential crime in ways that will enable them to apprehend the criminal in the act, or at least to cut short his crime almost as soon as it begins.

The community service model is variously called "team policing," the "beat commander project," the "basic car plan," or the "neighborhood police team." Variants of it have been tried in Syracuse, Los Angeles, New York, Cincinnati, Detroit, and elsewhere.[7] The essential idea is to assign a team of patrolmen and supervisors to a small area—say, one precinct or a few beats—and to leave them there with broad latitude to learn about the neighborhood, alter their own working hours to meet the demands of the area, conduct much of their own follow-up investigation on crimes, and serve as active intermediaries between citizens and various social service agencies. Instead of moving patrolmen about through many neighborhoods in response to radio calls for service, each team of patrolmen is expected to handle all the calls in their own neighborhood. Instead of turning all crime complaints, once the initial report is taken, over to detectives or other specialists from "downtown," the team is expected to do much of the initial investigation. The immediate objective is to develop among the officers a strong sense of territoriality—their beats are "their turf"—out of which will arise, it is hoped, a stronger sense of identification with the community and the fostering of reciprocity in information and service.

The crime attack model takes a much wider variety of forms, ranging from "Operation Identification" (designed to mark valuable items so as to simplify their recovery and thus discourage their theft) to stakeout squads stationed in the back rooms of liquor stores waiting for an armed robber to enter. In each case, the strategy is to make an object harder to steal or a thief easier to catch. Little effort goes into developing information from the community, because the police recognize that since the vast majority of citizens commit no serious crimes and know no serious criminals, they have little information to offer. A common crime attack tactic is the use of decoys—that is, officers disguised as derelicts, cab drivers, hippies, and other frequent targets of criminal activity. Some cities, such as New York, have used community service or team policing methods in some areas and decoys and stakeout squads in others.

Although there is no logical conflict, there sometimes appears to be tension between the two approaches. Stakeout squads and decoys may produce dead criminals rather than arrests. Decoys sometimes have difficulty convincing either criminals or innocent bystanders that they are police officers; indeed, there have even been instances in which a decoy has been unable to convince a fellow officer that he was a cop. As a result, police decoys have sometimes been attacked by citizens and shot at by skeptical officers. In racially tense areas, aggressive law enforcement, unless well managed, can give rise to community criticism.

At the same time, team policing may improve the morale of the officers or the image of the department without producing any increase in arrests or any decrease in crime. If crime rates are insensitive to the number of officers driving around on preventive patrol, they may also be unaffected by efforts to get to know the community.

So far, there has been virtually no independent evaluation of any crime-attack strategy, but statistics gathered by the police themselves seem encouraging. In 1971 the NYPD formed an "anticrime patrol" of about one thousand officers dressed in civilian clothes or in disguises who worked the streets of high-crime areas. The theory was that criminals recognize and avoid uniformed patrolmen (hence the ineffectiveness of random preventive patrol) and commit crimes that are infrequently solved by detectives. The objective of the NYPD effort was to catch criminals in the act. Although the plainclothes officers represented only about 5 per cent of the men and women assigned to each precinct, they made in 1973 over 18 per cent of the felony arrests, including over half the arrests for robbery and about 40 per cent of those for burglary and auto theft. Furthermore, three-fourths of these arrests resulted in convictions, far higher than the city-wide rate.[8] There is no way as yet, however, of determining with confidence the impact of these high arrest levels on crime rates.

Progress in evaluating the community service model has been somewhat greater. The most ambitious experiment of this kind ever done is underway in Cincinnati, where the police have implemented in District One (the downtown, inner-city area) a "Community Sector Team Policing Program," or COMSEC. Under COMSEC there was a slight increase (about 16 per cent) in police manpower assigned to District One, but a profound change in the way the police were organized and directed.

Formerly, motorized patrolmen in District One handled calls from throughout the area, even from a place outside their normal "sector" (i.e., beat). When particular problems arose, specialized units from headquarters were called in—to handle juveniles, burglary reports, narcotics, and so on. The patrolmen who took the initial call for service often performed no function beyond that of making a routine report. At the start of a tour of duty, the officers assigned to the district would muster together and listen to such information as a supervisor may have; much of it might not apply to their beat. There was little opportunity to exchange information in any systematic way with officers covering the same sector. Nor was there always a close correspondence between the number of officers on patrol in a sector and the workload at a given time in that sector. Finally, "community relations" was the responsibility of a community relations unit that worked out of headquarters. In all these respects, the Cincinnati police were organized in much the same way as other big-city police.

COMSEC changed much of that. Each sector in District One was now covered by a team that remained in that sector and handled almost all (91 per cent) of the calls for service from it. The team rarely called on specialized units for help on any matter except homicide. Not even the central traffic unit operates within District One except for some patrolling of the expressways. Detectives rarely appear. The Tactical Patrol Unit has been disbanded. Community relations became part of the ongoing responsibilities of each patrolman, to be discharged by involving local citizens in crime prevention and service activities. Officers on the beat appear at meetings in that neighborhood to answer questions and to gather information by, for example, showing pictures of known burglars operating in the area. Information developed by each officer is to be shared among his colleagues under the guidance of an information "collator." Working hours are changed frequently to adjust to actual workloads and neighborhood needs.

The eighteen-month experiment began in March 1973; six months later the preliminary results were analyzed by Alfred I. Schwartz of the Urban Institute. The total number of reported crimes decreased in Division One while it increased in the rest of the city. The greatest decrease in the experimental area was in the number of burglaries, which dropped by 7 per cent; in the rest of the city, burglaries increased by more than 2 per cent.

Curiously, citizen fears of crime were not greatly allayed by the COMSEC program. The proportion of those living in District One who felt unsafe when out alone at night did not change substantially; the proportion who thought their neighborhood more dangerous than others actually went up; the proportion—about half—who believed their chances of being robbed had gone up in the past few years did not change. And this lack of any greater sense of security was not the result of the invisibility of the police—there was a significant increase in the percentage of citizens in District One who reported having seen police officers walking the area. Nor was it the result of any lack of public confidence in the police—about 90 per cent of the citizens interviewed thought the police handling of various incidents was "good" or "very good." In fact, even among those *arrested* by the police, 80 per cent thought the officers were basically honest, and more than half thought they were properly respectful to persons such as themselves.

Another experiment, this one in Rochester, New York, suggests, on the basis of preliminary results, that one aspect of the team policing model may have another advantage—namely, improving police effectiveness in investigating crimes that have been reported. In Rochester, two or three teams were allowed to combine the patrol and investigative (or detective) functions, instead of having separate units do each, as in most departments. The theory was that immediate follow-up on crime reports by officers assigned to a neighborhood permanently would lead to more crimes being solved (or as the police put it, "cleared") than if the follow-up was done by detectives sent in some time later to work independently of the patrolmen.

After one year, outside evaluators, led by Peter Bloch of the Urban Institute, concluded that there had been an impressive increase in the number of crimes cleared by the experimental teams as compared to the number cleared in other parts of the city by conventional detective units. For example, Team A more than doubled the number of robberies and burglaries they were able to solve (from about 18 per cent before they started to about 35 per cent after) and more than quintupled the number of larcenies being cleared. By comparison, conventional police in a similar part of the city showed no improvement over the same period.

It is too early to tell whether these striking results will continue and can be confirmed by further study and experimentation. Above all, there is as yet no way of knowing whether improved police ability to solve crimes will affect the crime rate.

Some will find the last statement inexplicable. If more crimes are solved because more criminals are arrested, the crime rate *must* go down—or so one would suppose. In fact, police ability

95

to solve crimes may have very little affect on how many crimes are committed. The burglaries most easily solved may be random, impulsive crimes committed occasionally by amateurs; most burglaries may instead be committed by skilled professionals who are frequent violators and only rarely caught. Even more important, a criminal is not immobilized by an arrest, or at least not for long. Most are out on bail promptly—sometimes before the arresting officer can finish his paperwork. Trials are frequently delayed for months, convictions are not assured, and penalties may be light (e.g., probation). Finally, important social environmental changes, such as rapid population growth, the increase in the proportion of young persons, sharp movements in the business cycle, and abnormally hot or cold weather may have so much influence on the propensity to crime that gains resulting from police methods may be completely obscured.

At this stage of our understanding of police work it is hard to draw any comprehensive conclusions about the ability of the police to prevent crime that is not so guarded and cautious as to be useless. Since 1954, we have gathered more questions than answers. In general, however, these observations seem warranted:

First, a massive increase in police presence on foot in densely settled areas will probably lead to a reduction in those crimes, such as muggings and auto theft, that require the perpetrators to use the city streets. This seems to be supported by Operation 25, the manpower increase in the twentieth precinct, and the New York subway experience. No one can yet say with any confidence, however, how long this reduction will persist (except in the special case of the subway project, where it endured for many years), and how much crime is merely displaced to another location. The suggestion from the twentieth precinct that there is little displacement remains just that—only a suggestion, inadequately supported by data. And the cost of any massive increase is—well, massive.

Second, substantial increases in random preventive patrol by police in marked cars do not appear to have any affect on the crime rates, not do they tend to reassure the citizenry about their safety. Police time spent driving the streets waiting for something to happen is not time well spent.

Third, the community service model of neighborhood team policing appears, on the basis of preliminary results from Cincinnati, to be of some value in reducing burglaries even without massive increases in police manpower. Ironically, the effort by the police to get closer to the community has not as yet reassured the community about its safety or made much difference in what the community thinks about the police, or vice versa.

Fourth, a crime-attack strategy aimed at specific offenses may hold great promise, but so far it has been the least well-evaluated of all police methods. More careful work is needed in this area than in almost any other aspect of police behavior.

Finally, whatever may be the value of the police presence as a deterrent to crime, the value of the police as apprehenders of criminals is not something that the police alone are capable of improving. The value of an arrest for incapacitating a criminal or for deterring would-be criminals from following his example depends crucially on what the courts elect to do with the arrestee, and here there has been virtually no careful experimentation at all. A few police departments in this country have shown themselves to be remarkably innovative, experimental, and open to evaluative research. There are not as yet many prosecutors or courts about which one can say the same thing.

Chapter 6

The Police and
the Community

ONE of the chief constraints on the effectiveness of the police in dealing with crime is thought to arise out of their relations with the community they serve. It is not only that the police must perform for the community many tasks unrelated to law enforcement, but that the very effort to enforce the law will bring the police into conflict with the citizens they are supposed to serve, to the detriment of both. In this view, the citizens are fearful of and hostile toward the police, and the police reciprocate by displaying unjustified suspicion and harsh and even brutal behavior. The harder the police try to catch criminals, the more they are likely to rub raw the sores of community discontent.

During the 1960s, bad police-community relations were described as a chief cause of black riots. The police were variously described as an "army of occupation" and "pigs," the neighborhood residents as "rioters" and "lawless" or worse. At the height of the concern, it seemed as if the inner cities were in a perpetual state of war, and in some places that was not very far from the truth.

If matters were always and everywhere this bad, then nothing could be done. One cannot ameliorate with government programs a problem that arises out of the rejection of the legitimacy of government itself. If police and cities are, in the slums, implacable enemies utterly beyond reconciliation, then all the talk of improving matters with community relations programs, better trained officers, and more effective "communication" seems pointless and trivial.

In fact, police-community relations were neither so bad as the "war" theory proclaimed nor so good that we can dismiss the matter as a nonproblem. Furthermore, many of the favorite methods for improving police-community relations *are* either pointless or trivial, not because the problem they address is of catastrophic proportions, but for a much simpler and more common reason: They are based on a misunderstanding of the day-to-day relationships and attitudes that exist between the police and a poor neighborhood.

Citizen Views of the Police

THE SINGLE most striking fact about the attitudes of citizens, black and white, toward the police is that in general these attitudes are positive, not negative. A study done in 1964 of blacks living in several large cities showed that a majority of those interviewed in Atlanta, Chicago, and New York City thought the police treated blacks "very well" or "fairly well." [1] A study done for the President's Commission on Law Enforcement and Administration of Justice indicated that among several thousand men, the overwhelming majority of both whites and blacks believed that the police were "very good" or "pretty good" at being respectful to "persons like yourself." [2] A survey of residents of Washington, D.C., disclosed that among the persons who had reported having a recent contact with the police, 78 per cent thought the officer had acted properly.[3] In this study, 80 per cent of the black men said that the police "deserve a lot more respect and thanks than they get." [4] In two largely black precincts in Boston and Chicago, only 10 per cent of those citizens interviewed said that they had little or no respect for the way the police did their job.[5] Finally, a survey done for the Kerner commission indicated that about one-third of the blacks interviewed were critical of the police in their city (believing that the police use insulting language, that they search without reason, and that they rough people up unnecessarily), but not only was this group much less than a majority, it was also about the same size as the group that was critical of the mayor, the state government, the federal government, and local merchants.[6]

Of course, interpreting these findings depends a good deal on how big one thinks a third or a quarter is. With respect to the last study, for example, one could report it either as saying "two-thirds of the blacks were not critical of the police" or as saying "fully [or "a whopping"] one-third of the blacks were highly critical of the police." Whatever adjectives one chooses to append to these numbers, however, one thing is clear—they offer little support for the view that the great majority of blacks are seething with resentment against the police on grounds of injustice or abuse.

But if a majority of blacks are not critical of police conduct, a significant minority are, and this minority is composed chiefly of the young. A study of the Watts area of Los Angeles done shortly after the riot questioned persons of all ages about the police (among other things). It found that only 31 per cent of the blacks over the age of forty-five, but 60 per cent of those between the ages of fifteen and twenty-nine, thought there was some or a great deal of police brutality. Of the males under the age of thirty-five, over half claimed that they had been subjected to insulting language, almost half to a "roust, frisk, or search without good reason," and almost a quarter to "unnecessary force while being arrested." [7]

It is not surprising that young men, whether for good reason or not, should dislike the police. Most crimes, so far as we know, are committed by young men; brawls and rowdiness in which the police must intervene typically involve young males; riot participants tend to be youthful; complaints from citizens about neighborhood nuisances are often directed at the behavior of young men. In any community, black or white, rich or poor, the young man and the police are natural adversaries. The crucial question is whether young black males feel, rightly or wrongly, more aggrieved than their white counterparts. From such evidence as we have, the answer is that they do.

In a study for the Kerner commission nearly six thousand persons, black and white, living in fifteen large cities were interviewed. Their attitudes toward and experiences with the police were tabulated by race and age. The results are sufficiently interesting to warrant reporting in full. Tables 1, 2, and 3 show that at all age levels, blacks are more critical of the police than whites—that is, they are much more likely to believe that the police use insulting language, that they frisk and search for no reason, and that they rough people up. [8] In the youngest age group (sixteen to twenty), blacks are twice as likely as whites to have these beliefs, but in the older age groups they are *three or four* times as likely as whites to think this way. Stated another way, a sixty-five-year-old black has the same beliefs about the police as an eighteen-year-old white.

For both blacks and whites, beliefs critical of the police decline in frequency as one grows older, but the decline is greater for the whites. By the time they are about thirty-five years old, the great majority of blacks and whites do not have strong anti-police views, but while for the whites criticism is confined to a tiny fraction of the population (about one-tenth), for the blacks it remains the active concern of about a quarter or more.

TABLE 1
"Police Use Insulting Language"

AGE GROUP (BOTH SEXES)	BELIEVE IT HAS HAPPENED		HAPPENED TO THEM	
	WHITE	BLACK	WHITE	BLACK
16–19	24%	55%	14%	24%
20–29	24	45	11	19
30–39	14	37	7	14
40–49	13	36	3	15
50–59	9	26	6	7
60–69	8	24	3	5

TABLE 2
"Police Frisk and Search Without Good Reason"

AGE GROUP (BOTH SEXES)	BELIEVE IT HAS HAPPENED		HAPPENED TO THEM	
	WHITE	BLACK	WHITE	BLACK
16–19	25%	51%	12%	22%
20–29	15	43	5	18
30–39	7	33	2	11
40–49	9	32	2	9
50–59	7	28	1	4
60–69	4	24	1	8

TABLE 3
"Police Rough People Up Unnecessarily"

AGE GROUP (BOTH SEXES)	BELIEVE IT HAS HAPPENED		HAPPENED TO THEM	
	WHITE	BLACK	WHITE	BLACK
16–19	25%	49%	3%	8%
20–29	13	43	1	7
30–39	7	33	3	3
40–49	5	30	0	2
50–59	6	26	1	4
60–69	3	20	0	1

Experience with the police, unlike beliefs about them, follows a somewhat different pattern. In the youngest age group, about twice as many blacks as whites report that they personally experienced insulting police language, an unreasonable search, or a roughing up. Past the age of fifty, however, there is not much difference in white and black experience—only an infinitesimal fraction of both races claim to have been the victims of police malpractice. If this cross-section of current black opinion is any guide to how attitudes develop over time (and it may not be), then age does not produce a reconciliation between beliefs and experiences for blacks to the same extent that it does for whites. By the time whites are in their fifties, there are only trivial differences between the proportions reporting an antipolice belief and those reporting an antipolice experience (less than 10 per cent in both cases); at the same age, by contrast, the proportion of blacks with antipolice beliefs (20 to 28 per cent) continues to be larger than that with antipolice experiences (8 per cent or less).

It is easy to become preoccupied with black criticisms of alleged police abuse; it is easy to forget that there is as much or more black criticism of inadequate police protection and service. In the Kerner commission survey, for example, a majority of black respondents believed that the police "don't come quickly," and about one-fourth say that this slow response has happened to them. Moreover, these attitudes and experiences, unlike those concerning abuses, do *not* change much with age. About half of all blacks aged twenty to twenty-nine think the police are too slow; about half of those aged sixty to sixty-nine feel the same way. About a quarter of those aged twenty to twenty-nine say they have experienced a slow response; about a quarter of those aged sixty to sixty-nine say the same thing.[9]

The president's crime commission cited a number of studies showing that in many areas blacks view "crime in the streets" as one of the most important problems afflicting their neighborhood.[10] A *Fortune* magazine survey of three hundred urban blacks in 1967 indicated they felt the same way—"better police protection" was the most frequent *neighborhood* need mentioned (personal concerns, such as better jobs and schooling, had the highest priority).[11] In December 1968 the New York branch of the NAACP issued a report demanding a halt to "the reign of criminal terror in Harlem" and called for assigning more police to the area, placing armed guards in housing projects, handing out harsher sentences to those convicted, and disposing more swiftly of criminal cases. The author of the report told a reporter that "it is not police brutality that makes people afraid to walk the streets at night," it is "criminal brutality." [12] In Detroit the Urban League launched a community attack on crime that has attracted wide initial support among blacks and whites. One black leader spoke of the need for more policemen and sentences "that will disturb the criminal, shaking him from criminal acts." [13] In the National Opinion Research Center study of ten thousand citizens and their attitudes toward the police, black men at every income level were more likely to believe that the police were very good or pretty good at being "respectful to people like yourself" than they were to believe that the police did a very good or pretty good job at "giving protection to the people in the neighborhood." In both cases, the highest-income blacks—those earning over $10,000 a year—were the most critical.[14]

In sum, blacks are more likely than whites to be critical of the police on grounds of both abuse and inadequate protection. While criticism of inadequate protection is voiced by close to a majority of all blacks, criticism of police abuse is expressed by a minority of perhaps one-fourth to one-third, and experience of police abuse is confined to a very small minority. Antipolice attitudes are strongest among young black males. Older blacks are much less likely to report police abuses but just as likely to report inadequate protection, perhaps because an older person is less likely to come into contact with the police as a suspect but just as likely to come into contact with a criminal as his victim. Finally, there are growing indications of outspoken black demands for *more*, not less, police activity.

Police Views of the Citizen

THE VIEWS of many police officers seem to confirm the "war" theory of police-community relations. Data gathered at least as far back as 1960 suggest that most big-city officers see the citizenry as at best uncooperative and at worst hostile. For example, a majority of Chicago police sergeants questioned in 1960 and again in 1965 felt that civilians generally did not cooperate with the police, that the department did not have the respect of most citizens, that their civilian friends would criticize the department to their faces, and that most people obey the law only from fear of being caught.[15] The ongoing COMSEC experiment in Cincinnati has revealed that whereas 90 per cent of the citizens thought the police behaved well in incidents they had witnessed, 85 per cent of the officers thought the chances of being abused by the citizens were high.

In fact, as the previous section indicated, the majority of all citizens, and the vast majority of white citizens, have a generally good opinion of the police and are in favor of measures designed to help them. The apparent contradiction between actual citizen opinion and police perception of it stems, I believe, from the fact that the average patrolman in a big city is most frequently in contact not with the "average citizen," but with a relatively small number of persons who are heavy users of police services (willingly or unwillingly), and his view of citizen attitudes is strongly influenced by this experience. By the nature of his job, the police officer is disproportionately involved with the poor, the black, and the young—partly because young males, especially poor ones, are more likely to be involved in criminal activities and breaches of the peace, and partly because even the law-abiding poor (who are, after all, the majority of the poor) must rely on the police for a variety of services which middle-class families do not require or, if they require them, obtain from nonpolice sources. The police, for example, are routinely expected in poor areas to deal with family quarrels; in more affluent neighborhoods, such disputes are either less threatening to the participants or are kept out of public view.

In a study done for the Kerner commission, Peter H. Rossi and his colleagues at Johns Hopkins University interviewed over four hundred police officers working in largely black sections of eleven major cities. When asked in general terms what they felt was their major problem to be faced, more officers mentioned a lack of public support than any other factor.[16] Fifty-four per cent were dissatisfied with the respect they received from citizens; 30 per cent believed that the average citizen in these neighborhoods held them in contempt. But when the police were asked about the views of *particular groups* in the neighborhood, a different picture emerged. The vast majority (between 72 and 94 per cent) felt that older persons, storekeepers, school teachers, and whites were "on their side"; the police were divided as to whether most blacks saw them as friends, enemies, or were indifferent; a majority believed that most adolescents saw the police as enemies.[17]

Interestingly, black police officers (about a hundred were interviewed) had the same opinion as their white colleagues—to them, the chief source of hostile citizen attitudes was to be found, in increasing order of importance, among "most Negroes," "most young adults," and "most adolescents." [18] The black officers are generally more sympathetic to the problems of blacks than are white officers—they are much more likely to believe that blacks are badly treated by the city as a whole and by the police in particular—but their conception of the problems facing the police officer tends to be quite similar to that of their white colleagues.[19]

In sum, when questioned closely, the community and the police tend to agree as to the source of their difficulties, though clearly they disagree over who is to blame. The chief problem is to be found in the relations between young males, especially black young males, and ghetto police officers. But if this is true, why is there not a tacit alliance between older black residents, interested in better police protection and fearful of rising rates of crime (especially juvenile crime), and police officers who are also concerned about crime and who want "more cooperation" in ending it? In part, there is such a convergence of views; one night spent in a ghetto police precinct will provide graphic evidence of the extent to which the older black residents, especially the women, regularly turn to the police for help. But to a considerable degree the alliance is never forged, at least not to the extent one finds in a middle-class white suburb. The reasons are skin color and the conditions of ghetto life.

Blackness conceals, for some police officers, the important differences in social class and respectability among blacks. Because the urban lower class is today disproportionately black (just as it was once disproportionately Irish), a dark skin is to the police a statistically significant cue to social status, and thus to potential criminality. If arrest figures are to be believed, blacks are ten times as likely to commit a murder and eight times as likely to commit an assault as whites. The possibility that social class and family background, not race as such, explains these differences in rate is less apparent than the association between skin color and crime; understandably (though often injustly), a black skin is taken as grounds for police suspicion and therefore for questioning and frisking.

However race may contribute to police suspicions, it is not clear that it produces a discriminatory pattern in the proportion of suspicious persons who are arrested. During 1966, independent observers watched police-juvenile encounters in three large cities and noted that only 15 per cent resulted in an arrest. In comparable situations the police were no more likely to arrest the black than the white. One factor that made the situations noncomparable was the presence of a complainant, usually an adult. When a black adult was present when the police dealt with a black juvenile, an arrest was more likely than when the adult was absent—usually because black adults, unlike whites, were more likely to insist upon an arrest.[20]

Even if arrest decisions are made fairly, there is no denying the tensions produced by mutual suspicions. The conditions of ghetto life, especially the fact of residential segregation, intensify the problem by leading blacks of various classes, and thus of various degrees of law-abidingness, to live in close proximity. To the police, this heterogeneity makes it difficult to perceive and act upon relevant differences in social position. Because so many urban blacks live in or near high-crime areas, they may innocently become not only the victims of crime but also the objects of police suspicion.

This problem, serious in any case, becomes acute if the police feel themselves obliged to intensify their crime prevention activities. There are very few strategies by which the police can reduce crime rates—indeed, for some "private" crimes, such as murder, there is almost nothing they can do—but such strategies as they have require them to place a community under closer surveillance, and thus to multiply the occasions on which citizens are likely to be stopped, questioned, or observed. Inevitably, the great majority of the persons stopped will be innocent of any wrongdoing; inevitably, many of these innocent persons will believe the police are "harassing" them; inevitably, innocent blacks will believe that they are being "harassed" because of their race.

Thus, if the law-abiding majority in a black community demand "more police protection," they are likely to be calling for police activity that will increase the frequency of real or perceived police abuses. If, on the other hand, they demand an end to "police harassment," they are likely to be ending police practices that have some (no one knows how much) crime prevention value.

Citizen Attitudes and Crime Control

HOW CITIZENS feel about the police may be the result of either their experiences (as crime victims, arrestees, ticketed motorists, or witnesses), their general beliefs about police behavior (as gleaned from television, newspapers, and friends), or both. If their feelings derive mainly from experiences, then there is something the police can do about the problem; if they derive from the media, there is rather little that can be done. Unfortunately, the evidence we have so far does not permit a simple answer to the question.

The data in Tables 1, 2, and 3 suggest rather strongly that unfavorable *views* about the police are much more common, especially among young blacks, than unfavorable *experiences* with the police. There is thus a good deal of evidence consistent with the view that general beliefs, acquired from the media or friends, are very important in shaping attitudes toward the police. But there are also data that show the effect on citizen attitudes of first-hand experience with the police.

A follow-up study of citizens served by the Baltimore Police Department showed that when the officer who answered a citizen's call for assistance took the trouble to explain his actions and to describe what was likely to happen, and followed up the initial contact with additional effort (investigation, another call), the citizen (either black or white) later reported a more favorable attitude toward the police than was true when the officer seemed unconcerned about the victim.[21] A similar finding was reported from a survey of residents of Seattle: Of those who had called the police to report a crime, the citizens who were satisfied with the way the police responded expressed more favorable general attitudes about the police than those who were dissatisfied.[22]

Getting a traffic ticket, on the other hand, appears to make little difference in citizen attitudes toward the police. The Seattle study found no relationship between such attitudes and whether a person had been ticketed in the preceding year, except for very low-income persons.[23] No doubt those of us who are ticketed often feel momentarily chagrined or irritated, but this seems to have no lasting effect on our attitudes toward the police.

Though citizen experiences with the police (except for most

traffic violations) affect citizen attitudes toward the police, they do not fully explain them. In the Baltimore study, for example, blacks were more critical of the police even when they reported that they had been treated the same as whites—that is, when they said the police responded promptly and handled the complaint satisfactorily.[24] In these cases, they may be expressing a view of the police that is more a product of the general burdens under which blacks have labored in our society.

Though one might presume that attitudes critical of the police impede law enforcement and order maintenance, this widespread belief is difficult to confirm with any systematic evidence. One way to test the theory is to ask whether persons with a low opinion of the police are less likely to call on them for help than persons who hold a high opinion. Obviously, if people refuse to call the police because of their attitudes toward them, then these attitudes are a major impediment to law enforcement. In two separate studies, however, the findings failed to support the theory; in each case, there was no difference in willingness to call the police between those citizens with favorable and unfavorable attitudes.[25]

Nor do sharp differences in the perceived quality of the local police department seem to make much difference in how citizens evaluate police fairness. In one of the studies done for President Johnson's crime commission, people were interviewed in two cities. One had a "traditional" police force with older patrolmen, a decentralized administrative structure, poor equipment and facilities, low pay, few blacks on the force, almost no community relations program, and weak internal discipline. The other was nationally famous for its "modernized," "professional" style with young patrolmen, good pay, highly centralized administration, an active internal inspection and discipline system, a large community relations program, and a high proportion of blacks serving in the ranks. In each city, residents of a predominantly black area were interviewed. The results showed that the citizens were aware of the kind of department they had—in the professional city only 18 per cent thought that the police were not doing a good job, while in the traditional city 35 per cent had this view. And when storekeepers in the area were asked how fast the police would respond to a call, only 19 per cent of those in the traditional city but 40 per cent of those in the professionalized city believed the police would arrive in less than five minutes.

But when asked how they evaluated the fairness, honesty, and abusiveness of the two forces, the citizens of the two communities displayed little difference in attitude. In both places 43 per cent said that being black means a difference in how you are treated by the police; in both cities 10 per cent said that they had little respect for the police; in both cities 16 per cent said they had seen the police use unnecessary force. Slightly more persons in the professionalized city (53 per cent) had "great respect" for the police than did residents of the traditional city (43 per cent), but the difference was not large.[26] The head of the professionalized department may wonder whether his efforts have been worth the candle—either he had improved the department but the citizens did not realize it or the "improvements" had not affected the behavior of patrolmen.

For their part, the police are convinced that lack of citizen cooperation and support is a major barrier to crime control. Any patrolman can recount many stories of an investigation being frustrated because bystanders claimed they "saw nothing," witnesses refused to testify, victims dropped charges, and no one would come to an officer's aid when he was being overpowered in a scuffle. To the police, a suspicious and skeptical attitude in dealing with citizens is amply justified by the facts, however that attitude might be interpreted by those who observe it.

The tension and dissatisfaction that characterize some police-citizen encounters arise out of the differing definitions of the situation held by officer and citizen. The most common calls for police help involve domestic disturbances and property losses (e.g., burglaries). In a disturbance, the citizen wants a "solution" that vindicates his "rights"; the officer sees only a conflict for which he can supply no solution and in which who has what

111

rights is quite unclear. The citizen views the police as an all-purpose emergency service; the officer is acutely aware of the differences between civil and criminal matters, of the impropriety of his intervening authoritatively in purely private ones, and of his inability to command or even influence the delivery of other public services.[27] In a property crime, the citizen wants his television set back, but the officer knows he is not likely to find it. The former wishes to see a prompt and vigorous investigation; the latter has no leads on which to base such an investigation and no time or resources with which to develop them. In both these cases, the citizen wants "action" but gets instead aloofness and apparent indifference. The officer wants peace and an orderly supply of information but confronts instead conflict, emotion, and confusion.

In short, the sources of police-citizen antagonisms are inherent in the situation and not the product of—though they may be exacerbated by—the accidental personal qualities and attitudes of either citizen or officer. The police see conflict and unrecoverable losses where the citizen expects vindication and restitution, and all of this under circumstances that make certain citizens—young males, especially black ones—particularly suspect. It is easy to see why each side concludes that the problem arises out of the moral failings of the other: "insensitive" or "bigoted" police, "disorderly" and "belligerent" citizens.

Some Nonsolutions

FOR MANY years, some well-meaning but probably mistaken efforts have been made to improve police-community relations by various expedients which have in common the defect of being based on a misconception of the problem. Consider, for example, the effort to find "better" officers, which in practice has meant officers with more education, preferably up through college.

A plausible case can be made for this view. Even if college teaches a man nothing of value in police work, it has two useful side effects: First, it selects from the general population men who have certain qualities (motivation, self-discipline, general intelligence) that are probably quite useful in a police career; second, it inculcates certain characteristics (civility, urbanity, self-control) that might be especially desirable in an officer. It is a measure of our ignorance in these matters that an equally plausible case to the contrary can be made. Recruiting college men will reduce substantially (at least for the time being) the chances of adding more blacks and other minority groups to the police forces, for they are underrepresented in college classes. While college may make a man civil (though recent campus disturbances suggest that effect is not quite universal), it also gives him (or reenforces for him) his sense of duty. This has led some college-trained officers to be excessively aggressive and arrest-prone when a gentler hand might be better. Moreover, college men may not be able to identify easily with or understand the problems of lower- and working-class persons with whom they must deal. Finally, a police career is most unattractive for a college man—the work of a patrolman is routine, sometimes dull, frequently unpleasant, and occasionally dangerous. One study in New York City showed that patrolmen with a college education display a higher degree of cynicism and a greater sense of deprivation than those with less education.[28] In sum, the value of college training is still largely a matter of conjecture.

Better training for men on the force is always recommended. There can be little doubt that the training now received is often perfunctory, partly as a result of inadequate programs and partly as a result of the desperate need for additional men—a need that has led some departments to put rookies on the street before their academy course is completed. But even assuming lengthy preservice training, "human relations" is inevitably that part of the curriculum with the least direct effect on the policemen. The law of arrest, or first aid, or the use of weapons can be taught by lecture and demonstration, but management of personal relations in tense situations is not so easily taught. It is the universal testimony of the officers I have interviewed that training-room discussions of minority groups and police-community relations have little impact, and that such impression as they produce quickly evaporates when the officer goes on the street and first encounters hostile or suspicious behavior. The officer may remember what he is *not* supposed to do ("don't address blacks with a racially insulting name such as 'boy' "), but he has precious little guidance as to what he *should* do when confronted by a serious verbal challenge to his authority.

If conventional training methods are of little value in this area, is it possible to develop unconventional, more intensive techniques that will work a more profound change in the attitude of the officer? Some departments have experimented with "sensitivity training" designed to produce heightened self-awareness and even significant personality changes. Such methods are based on group discussions, stimulated but not directed by a training leader, in which the participants criticize one another and reexamine themselves in prolonged and often emotional sessions.[29] Sometimes only police officers participate in such sessions; in other experiments, police and community residents participate together. One of the chief purposes of sensitivity training is to change the participants' orientation toward authority and its exercise so that they will engage in cooperative problem solving, rather than struggle to win superiority or maintain personal autonomy.

Unfortunately, the effects on organizational behavior generally of such training (actually, reeducation) methods have not been carefully studied, and the effects on police organization and behavior in particular have scarcely been studied at all. Though there are many enthusiasts for these techniques, and though their enthusiasm may derive from personal experience in seeing people changed, the empirical evidence that desirable change can be induced in organizations as a whole on a lasting basis and without important sacrifices in other values (such as goal attainment, productivity, or equity) is either nonexistent or equivocal.[30] And there are reasons to suppose that police work may be an especially refractory target for these methods. The patrolman, after all, is not regularly engaged in problem solving with familiar colleagues in a common organization; he is engaging in enforcing the law and settling disputes among strangers, many of whom are fearful or hostile, and some of whom may be dangerous. Conflict is not a figment of either party's imagination; it is real and serious (though either party may exaggerate it and thereby unnecessarily exacerbate it). And the patrolman typically works alone, or in pairs, and not as part of supportive organizations.

Finally, conventional police-community relations theory assigns a high priority to community organization. In many cities the police have organized a community relations bureau, with officers working either out of headquarters or precinct stations to meet with civic, minority, and neighborhood organizations and to stimulate new activities, especially those involving young people. Some departments have formed neighborhood councils or committees with which senior officers regularly meet to discuss grievances and problems.

The communications strategy is exemplified by the activities of one large midwestern police department. A study of its "district community workshops" discovered that the value of such meetings depended on the character ot the neighborhood.[31] In a high-crime-rate area inhabited by both well-to-do whites living in high-rise apartments and lower-income blacks in public housing projects, a workshop meeting was well attended (about two hundred people) by both whites and blacks, but all were adults—there were few young people, especially young blacks, present. There was a cooperative and constructive discussion with the police on how to solve vice and crime problems, especially those in the public housing projects. Plans were announced for assigning patrolmen to "vertical patrols" in the projects. Everyone left feeling that something useful had been accomplished.

In another neighborhood, populated by university students and poor blacks, the workshop meeting was a fiasco. The young *did* attend (about a hundred), mostly to complain about the police handling of a student demonstration. The police refused to answer questions, claiming that the matter was before the courts and thus they were enjoined from speaking about it. The blacks soon became disgusted with the haggling over the demonstration; they cared little about antiwar protest, they said, but cared greatly about the high crime rate in their neighborhood and about the "disrespectful" manner of the police. The three-corner shouting match—students, police, and blacks—broke up in confusion and bitterness.

In a third district, the crime rate was low. Middle- and upper-middle-class whites and blacks lived in a peaceful community and had little interest in police issues. Only thirty persons appeared for the workshop meeting and few raised any crime or police issues. There were complaints, but not ones to which the police could respond, regarding garbage collection, parking regulations, dogs running loose. Few community leaders were in attendance; most of the audience was composed of chronic complainers, each of whom was irritated by the need to sit through everybody else's account of *his* problem. The meeting ended with little sense of accomplishment.

That the workshop strategy worked well in one district suggests that it is worth doing; that it did not work well in two others indicates that its limits should be clearly recognized. (Some will argue that it is of no value at all if it only reaches middle-class persons, especially adults, but it is hard to understand why the concern of adults for more police protection is any less worthy of being served than the concern of young people for less police abuse.) Efforts to reach the young and those with lower income, at least by the communications approach, are exceptionally difficult and perhaps impossible. One first-hand account of such an effort is typical of many. A group of young black "street corner" males was enrolled in a job-preparation program in a west coast city. As the author describes it, the men were "cool"—they spoke in the hip vernacular, wore sunglasses indoors, and were dressed in loud (but inexpensive) clothes. Most were school dropouts. Many had police records. They were paid five dollars a day to be in the training program.

Almost daily the men spoke of "police brutality." All wanted to meet a representative of the police. One finally came, a sergeant from the community relations bureau. He was almost immediately "put down," with angry questions about "why you cats always kicking cats' asses" and detailed personal horror stories of experiences with the police. The sergeant could not get in a word. The next day a deputy chief appeared to try his hand at improving "communications." He, too, was besieged with stories of alleged brutality. He asked the men if they had filed complaints; none had. The chief asked why not. The men responded that if they did, "we would just get our asses kicked harder by the cop next time." The chief insisted that complaints would be fairly investigated. The men were not satisfied. One asked: "Okay man, you pretty smart. If I smack my buddy here upside the head and he files a complaint, what you gonna do?"

"Arrest you," the chief replied.

"Cool. Now let's say one of your ugly cops smacks *me* upside the head and I file a complaint—what you gonna do?"

"Investigate the complaint," the chief said. If it were true, the police would "take action" and "probably suspend" the officer.

"Well," the black rejoined, "how come *we* get arrested and *you* only get investigated?"

Efforts to distinguish between private resort to violence, for which there is no justification, and official use of violence, for which there may be, were to no avail. The chief was shouted down and finally left.[32]

Better-designed or more protracted efforts might produce more constructive communication between "hip" young black males and the police, but the gains, however worthwhile, are likely to be slight, for the problem is not fundamentally one of "communication." There is genuine conflict between the youths, who want to be left alone, and the police, who regard the young (rightly) as the chief source of crime and disorder, and who seek by various means, some proper and some improper, to control them—often on behalf of older blacks who want "better police protection."

The issue of "community control" of the police has of late come to dominate any discussion of police-community relations, just as a few years ago such a discussion focused largely on "civilian review boards." The argument is that both better police protection and better police conduct can only be insured by giving neighborhoods control over their own police. In this way, the police will be responsive to the needs of the local citizens—the community will develop both policies for the exercise of police discretion and methods for the restraint or correction of police misconduct.

It is difficult to evaluate this policy since, to a great extent, it is a slogan rather than a program. Its adherents believe fervently in it without being able to offer a very clear understanding of what might be involved. And since shifting authority over the police from city hall to the neighborhoods is perhaps the most far-reaching change that could be made in police practice, it is especially important that one examine it closely. "Community control" could vary from having neighborhood groups choose, or consent to the choice of, the police captain assigned to their precincts, to the creation of neighborhood police policy boards that would exercise day-to-day supervision over the policies and actions of officers assigned to a particular locale, and beyond even to organizing the neighborhood so that it could hire, train, and deploy its own independent police force. And the range of control could vary from control over local beat patrolmen (leaving specialized units, such as traffic or even the detectives, centrally managed) to control over all aspects of police work in the area.

Whatever the form of the community control proposals, however, certain questions can be asked that are generally applicable. The first, and perhaps most important, is whether in a period of exceptional tension between whites and blacks living in central cities, the various neighborhoods making up those cities should be given control over their own police forces. If any one neighborhood obtains control over its police, all other neighborhoods will be able to make similar demands. With feelings running high over school integration and busing, the prospects for peace are not likely to be enhanced by Balkanizing the city, equipping each area with its own police force, and letting the disputants, thus armed, settle their differences as best they can.

Second, the question of "community control" assumes that "community" exists and its will can be made effective in police matters. But, as suggested in Chapter 2, it is precisely in inner-city areas where community in a meaningful sense is likely to be lacking. It is because of the *absence* of "community"—i.e., of shared, spontaneously enforced values—that crime control and police-citizen relations are so difficult. Furthermore, in such neighborhoods the most active and influential factions are often those most inclined to exacerbate and exploit tensions, assert the most extravagant claims, and harass in the rawest manner the employees of whatever government agency operates in that area. Such factions are by no means representative of community opinion, and yet they often tend to dominate discussions and preempt the leading positions. Rank-and-file citizens who have more sober and genuine concerns over crime and police behavior may not be brought to power by "community control"; quite the contrary, their voices may be the ones most likely to be silenced rather than amplified.

Finally, plunging the police into a political arena in which the most emotional and provincial concerns set the tone for decision making is not likely to ease the problem of recruiting and holding able men for the force. A major concern of the patrolman arises from the inconsistent expectations and contrary authorities that now define his task—his superiors, "politicians," the public all provide him with various and conflicting definitions of his function, usually (it seems to him) by criticism after the fact. Subordinating him to community councils that regularly and variously debate his role is not likely to increase his sense of confidence or the attractiveness of a police career.[33]

More Promising Prospects

WE ARE only beginning to learn whether there are better changes that could be made. A good deal of thought has been given to ways of identifying men and women who will make good police officers, which is to say persons who can handle the ambiguities of the situations they confront and the various challenges to their personal authority in a reasonable and constructive manner. The chief difficulty has been in specifying, precisely and in advance of recruitment, just what these qualities are. Once we are confident about that, there can be little doubt that ways will be found to screen out recruits who lack these qualities. Analyses carried out in New York City suggest that troublesome recruits can often be identified either before joining the force or during their training and probationary period.[34] Then the problem will become one of finding the administrative and political capacity to insure that poor prospects, once spotted, can be dropped from the force before they achieve what is, thanks to civil service, virtually permanent possession of their jobs.

Once selected, the recruit must be properly trained. Most training programs I have observed emphasize memorization of legal codes and departmental rules more than development of skills at managing social conflict. And familiarization with the law, which is of course important, is done inefficiently (by lectures) rather then efficiently (by programmed, individualized instruction). Furthermore, the precinct or station house socialization process that occurs after the recruit leaves the academy probably fails to reenforce the desirable aspects of recruit training, and may in fact lead the recruit to believe that his formal training should be discredited or ignored.

It is easy to misunderstand the problem. What is necessary is *not* to replace training for police work with training for social work, *not* to separate order-maintenance and law-enforcement responsibilities, *not* to substitute "human relations skills" for the ability to make an arrest or take charge of a situation. The debate over the role of the patrolman has tended to obscure the fact that the patrolman does all of these things most of the time—though the law-enforcement, order-maintenance, and service-provision aspects of his task can be analytically distinguished, concretely they are thoroughly intermixed. Even in a routine law-enforcement situation (e.g., arresting a fleeing purse snatcher), how the officer deals with the victim and the onlookers at the scene is often as important as how he handles the suspect. The victim and onlookers, after all, are potential witnesses who may have to testify in court; assuring their cooperation is as necessary as catching the person against whom they will testify. The argument about whether "cops" should be turned into "social workers" is a false one, for it implies that society can exercise some meaningful choice over the role the patrolman should play. Except at the margin, it cannot; what it can do is attempt to prepare officers for the complex role they now perform.

The legal code is not irrelevant to performing this role, but neither does it always provide an unambiguous cue as to the correct course of action. And even when it does provide such a cue, the other elements of the situation (for example, challenges to the officer's authority or self-respect) may obscure that cue.

A recruitment program must have the tested capacity to identify persons who can handle calmly challenges to their self-respect and manhood, are able to tolerate ambiguous situations, have the physical capacity to subdue persons, are able to accept responsibility for the consequences of their own actions, can understand and apply legal concepts in concrete situations, and are honest.

A training program should develop each of the above abilities by means of instruction in situations that simulate as far as possible real-world conditions. The object should be to develop an inner sense of competence and self-assurance so that, under conditions of stress, conflict, and uncertainty, the officer is capable of responding flexibly and in a relatively dispassionate manner rather than rigidly, emotionally, or defensively. These objectives will not be attained by simply multiplying courses that, seriatim, take up the law, departmental rules, unarmed combat, and "human relations." There is, of course, a growing awareness of the social and psychological aspects of police work, but lectures on such topics and the scrutiny of texts that urge the reader to become aware of how others perceive him are hardly adequate.

The training conditions must be designed to place officers in situations of stress and conflict in which they must manage their own behavior and that of others in a manner consistent with (but rarely determined by) legal standards. Generating such situations in the classroom is not simple, but the efforts of some departments have shown that it can be done in ways that lead the students involved to experience genuine emotions, lose their tempers, and feel threatened.[35] By observing the behavior of others and by hearing comments on their own behavior in these situations, the recruit can better learn what he can expect from others and (most importantly) from himself in real-life situations. If a way can also be found to continue this process of self-awareness and supervised behavior after being assigned to his first patrol duty, the patrolman's training can be made continuous rather than (as is now the case) sharply segmented into often inconsistent "academy" and "street" phases.

Finally, the properly recruited and trained officer has to be placed in an organizational role that maximizes his chances of being able to work collaboratively with those parts of the community he serves that want and welcome his presence. This is the most difficult of all the changes that are required; it is hard to devise the best strategy and easy to become discouraged at the small gains that result. The various "team policing" experiments underway in a number of cities are the best-known efforts in this direction, but as indicated in Chapter 5, the benefits in either crime control or community relations cannot yet be established beyond reasonable doubt.

Properly trained and organized, the police may even help evoke a sense of community and a capacity for self-regulation where none is now found. This is the significance, I believe, of the various community security patrols now found in public housing projects and big-city neighborhoods. Not only do they place more eyes and ears on the street and supply escort services for women coming home from supermarkets and bus stops, they can, if both local police and citizen patrols are wisely led, produce a belief that crime control and order maintenance are the joint responsibility of officers and citizens, and that collaborative ventures to this common end are possible.

More attention will have to be given to the costs and benefits of various police methods, such as routine "street stops" to question suspicious pedestrians and drivers. There is no doubt that many of those stopped resent it, though some of the resentment may result from the manner in which it is done rather than the fact of its being done.[36] There is also no doubt that the police frequently find fugitives or contraband by this method. Observers for the crime commission, for example, reported that out of three hundred eight searches by the police, weapons or stolen property were found on about one-fourth of the persons and in over half of the premises.[37] The issue thus becomes one of balancing the gains to law enforcement from the costs to community relations. If, as is likely, some stops under some circumstances are judged to be proper and worthwhile, then a good deal of attention should be given to defining those circumstances and training officers to carry out those stops with civility.

Even under the best of circumstances, however, there are limits to how much can be done. There is a fundamental, and to a degree inescapable, conflict between strategies designed to cut street crime (saturation patrols, close surveillance) and those designed to minimize tensions (avoid "street stops," reduce surveillance, ignore youth groups). Ultimately, the best way to minimize tensions is to find nonpolice methods for reducing street crime. To the extent that better economic opportunities, speedier court dispositions, more effective sentencing decisions, and improved correctional methods can reduce street crime, the burdens on the police and the tensions between police and citizen can be greatly reduced.

Chapter 7

Heroin

IT HAS BEEN widely believed that much of the increase in predatory crime is the result of heroin addicts supporting their habits; that heroin use has become a middle-class white as well as lower-class black phenomenon of alarming proportions; and that conventional law-enforcement efforts to reduce heroin use have not only failed but may in fact be contributing to the problem by increasing the cost of the drug for the user, leading thereby to the commission of even more crimes and the corruption of even more police officers. These generally held opinions have led to an intense debate over new policy initiatives to deal with heroin, an argument usually described as one between advocates of a "law-enforcement" policy (which includes shutting off opium supplies in Turkey and heroin-manufacturing laboratories in France and Mexico, arresting more heroin dealers in the United States, and using civil commitment procedures, detoxification centers, and methadone maintenance programs) and partisans of a "decriminalization" policy (which includes legalization of the use or possession of heroin, at least for adults, and distribution of heroin to addicts at low cost, or zero cost, through government-controlled clinics).

The intensity of the debate tends to obscure the fact that most of the widely accepted opinions on heroin use are not supported by much evidence; that the very concept of "addict" is ambiguous and somewhat misleading; and that many of the apparently reasonable assumptions about heroin use and crime—such as the assumption that the legalization of heroin would dramatically reduce the rate of predatory crime, or that intensified law enforcement drives the price of heroin up, or that oral methadone is a universal substitute for heroin, or that heroin use spreads because of the activities of "pushers" who can be identified as such—turn out on closer inspection to be unreasonable, unwarranted, or at least open to more than one interpretation.

"Punitive" versus "Medical" Approaches

MOST IMPORTANT, the current debate has failed to make explicit, or at least to clarify, the philosophical principles underlying the competing positions. Those positions are sometimes described as the "punitive" versus the "medical" approaches, but these labels are of little help. For one thing, they are far from precise: Putting an addict in jail is certainly "punitive," but putting him in a treatment program, however benevolent its intentions, may be seen by him as no less "punitive." Shifting an addict from heroin to methadone may be "medical" if he makes the choice voluntarily—but is it so if the alternative to methadone maintenance is a criminal conviction for heroin possession? And while maintaining an addict on heroin (as is done in Great Britain and as has been proposed for the United States) is not "punitive" in any legal sense, neither is it therapeutic in any medical sense. Indeed, there seem to be no forms of therapy that will "cure" addicts in any large numbers of their dependence on heroin. Various forms of intensive psychotherapy and group-based "personality restructuring" may be of great value to certain drug users, but by definition they can reach only very small numbers of persons, and perhaps only for limited periods of time.

But the fundamental problem with these and other labels is that they avoid the central question: Does society have only the right to protect itself (or its members) from the harmful acts of heroin users, or does it have in addition the responsibility (and thus the right) to improve the well-being (somehow defined) of heroin users themselves? In one view, the purpose of the law is to insure the maximum amount of liberty for everyone, and an action of one person is properly constrained by society if—and only if—it has harmful consequences for another person. This is the utilitarian conception of the public interest and, when applied to heroin use, it leads such otherwise unlike men as Milton Friedman, Herbert Packer, and Thomas Szasz to oppose the use of criminal sanctions for heroin users. The late Professor Packer, for example, wrote that a desirable aspect of liberalism is that it allows people "to choose their own roads to hell if that is where they want to go."

In another view, however, society has an obligation to enhance the well-being of each of its citizens even with respect to those aspects of their lives that do not directly impinge on other people's lives. In this conception of the public good, all citizens of a society are bound to be affected—indirectly but perhaps profoundly and permanently—if a significant number are permitted to go to hell in their own way. A society is therefore unworthy if it permits, or is indifferent to, any activity that renders its members inhuman or deprives them of their essential (or "natural") capacities to judge, choose, and act. If heroin use is such an activity, then its use should be proscribed. Whether that proscription is enforced by mere punishment or by obligatory therapy is a separate question.

The alternative philosophical principles do not necessarily lead to diametrically opposed policies. A utilitarian might conclude, for example, that heroin use is so destructive of family life that society has an interest in proscribing it (though he is more likely, if experience is any guide, to allow the use of heroin and then deal with its effect on family life by advocating social services to "help problem families"). And a moralist might decide that though heroin should be illegal, any serious effort to enforce that law against users would be so costly in terms of other social values (privacy, freedom, the integrity of officialdom) as not to be worth it, and he thus might allow the level of enforcement to fall to a point just short of that at which the tutelary power of the law would be jeopardized. Still, even if principles do not determine policies uniquely, thinking clearly about the former is essential to making good judgments about the latter. And to think clearly about the former, it is as important to ascertain the effects of heroin on the user as it is to discover the behavior of a user toward society.

The User

THERE IS no single kind of heroin user. Some persons may try it once, find it unpleasant, and never use it again; others may "dabble" with it on occasion but, though they find it pleasurable, will have no trouble stopping; still others may use it on a regular basis but in a way that does not interfere with their work. But some persons, who comprise a large (if unknown) percentage of all those who experiment with heroin, develop a relentless and unmanageable craving for the drug such that their life becomes organized around searching for it, using it, enjoying it, and searching for more. Authorities differ on whether all such persons—whom I shall call "addicts," though the term is not well defined and its scientific status is questionable—are invariably physiologically dependent on the drug, as evidenced by painful "withdrawal" symptoms that occur whenever they cease using it. Some persons may crave the drug without being dependent, others may be dependent without craving it. We need not resolve these definitional and medical issues, however, to recognize that many (but not all) heroin users are addicts in the popular sense of the term.

No one knows how many users of various kinds there are, at what rate they have been increasing in number, or of what happens to them at the end of their "run." That they have increased in number is revealed, not only by the testimony of police and narcotics officers, but by figures on deaths attributed to heroin. Between 1967 and 1971, the number of deaths in Los Angeles County attributed to heroin use more than tripled, and although improved diagnostic skills in the coroner's office may account for some of this increase, it does not (in the opinion of the University of Southern California student task force report) account for it all. A Harvard student task force used several techniques to estimate the size of the heroin-user population in Boston, and concluded that there was a tenfold increase in the decade of the 1960s. Why that increase occurred, and whether it will continue, are matters about which one can only speculate. The USC group estimated that there are at least fifty thousand addicts in Los Angeles; the Harvard group estimated that there are six thousand in Boston; various sources conventionally refer (with what accuracy we do not know) to the "hundred thousand" addicts in New York.[1]

No one has proposed a fully satisfactory theory to explain the apparent increase in addiction. There are at least four speculative possibilities, some or all of which may be correct. The rise in real incomes during the prosperity of the 1960s may simply have made possible the purchase of more heroin as it made possible the purchase of more automobiles or color television sets. The cult of personal liberation among the young may have led to greater experimentation with heroin as it led to greater freedom in dress and manners and the development of a rock music culture. The war in Vietnam may have both loosened social constraints and given large numbers of young soldiers easy access to heroin supplies and ample incentive (the boredom, fears, and demoralization caused by the war) to dabble in the drug. Finally, the continued disintegration of the lower-income, especially black, family living in the central city may have heightened the importance of street peer groups to the individual, and thus (in ways to be discussed later in this chapter) placed him in a social environment highly conducive to heroin experimentation. There are, in short, ample reasons to suppose (though few facts to show) that important changes in both the supply of and demand for heroin occurred during the last decade.

Heavy users of heroin, according to their own testimony, tend to be utterly preoccupied with finding and consuming the drug. Given an unlimited supply (that is, given heroin at zero cost), an addict will "shoot up" three to five times a day. Given the price of heroin on the black market—currently about $20 a bag, with varying numbers of bags used in each fix—some addicts may be able to shoot up only once or twice a day. The sensations associated with heroin use by most novice addicts are generally the same: keen anticipation of the fix, the "rush" when the heroin begins to work in the bloodstream, the euphoric "high," the drowsy or "nodding" stage as the "high" wears off, and then the beginnings of the discomfort caused by the absence of heroin. For the veteran addict the "high" may no longer be attainable, except perhaps at the risk of a lethal overdose. For him, the sensations induced by heroin have mainly to do with anesthetizing himself against withdrawal pain—and perhaps against most other feelings as well—together with a ritualistic preoccupation with the needle and the act of injection.

The addict is intensely present-oriented. Though "dabblers" or other episodic users may save heroin for a weekend fix, the addict can rarely save any at all. Some, for example, report that they would like to arise in the morning with enough heroin for a "wake-up" fix, but almost none have the self-control to go to sleep at night leaving unused heroin behind. Others report getting enough heroin to last them for a week, only to shoot it all the first day. How many addicts living this way can manage a reasonably normal family and work life is not known, but clearly many cannot. Some become heroin dealers in order to earn money, but a regular heavy user seldom has the self-control to be successful at this enterprise for long. Addicts turned dealers frequently report a sharp increase in their heroin use as they consume much of their sales inventory.

It is this craving for the drug, and the psychological states induced by its use, that are the chief consequences of addiction; they are also the most important consequences about which one must ultimately have a moral or political view, whatever the secondary effects of addiction produced by current public policy. At the same time, one should not suppose that all of these secondary effects can be eliminated by changes in policy. For example, while there are apparently no specific pathologies—serious illnesses or physiological deterioration—that are known to result from heroin use per se, the addict does run the risk of infections caused by the use of unsterile needles, poisoning as a result of shooting an overdose (or a manageable dose that has been cut with harmful products), and thrombosed veins resulting from repeated injections.[2] Some of these risks could be reduced if heroin were legally available in clinics operated by physicians, but they could not be eliminated unless literally everyone wishing heroin were given it in whatever dosage, short of lethal, he wished. In Great Britain, where pure heroin is legally available at low prices, addicts still have medical problems arising out of their use of the drug—principally unsterile self-injections, involuntary overdoses, and voluntary overdoses (that is, willingly injecting more than they should in hopes of obtaining a new "high"). If, as will be discussed below, heroin were injected under a doctor's supervision (as it is not in England), the risk of sepsis and of overdoses would be sharply reduced—but at the cost of making the public heroin clinic less attractive to addicts who wish to consume not merely a maintenance dose but a euphoria-producing (and therefore risky) one.

Why Heroin?

NO GENERALLY accepted theory supported by well-established facts exists to explain why only some persons become addicts. It is easy to make a list of factors that increase (statistically, at least) the risk of addiction: Black males living in low-income neighborhoods, coming from broken or rejecting families, and involved in "street life" have much higher chances of addiction than upper-middle-class whites in stable families and "normal" occupations. But some members of the latter category do become addicted, and many members of the former category do not; why this should be the case, no one is sure. It is easy to argue that heroin use occurs only among people who have serious problems (and thus to argue that the way to end addiction is to solve the underlying problems), but in fact many heavy users seem to have no major problems at all. Isidor Chein and his coworkers in their leading study of addiction in New York found that between one-quarter and one-third of addicts seemed to have no problems for which heroin use was a compensation.[3]

Though we cannot predict with much confidence who will and who will not become an addict, we can explain why heroin is used and how its use spreads. The simple fact is that heroin use is intensely pleasurable, for many people more pleasurable than anything else they might do. Heroin users will have experimented with many other drugs, and when heroin is hard to find they may return to them or to alcohol, but for the vast majority of users heroin remains the drug of choice. The nature of the pleasure will vary from person to person—or, perhaps, the interpretive description of that pleasure will vary—but the desire for it remains the governing passion of the addicts' lives. All of us enjoy pleasure; an addict is a person who has found the supreme pleasure and the means to make that pleasure recur.

This fact helps explain why "curing" addiction is so difficult (virtually impossible for many addicts) and how new addicts are recruited. Addicts sent to state or federal hospitals to be detoxified—i.e., to be withdrawn from heroin use—almost invariably return to such use after their release, simply because using it is so much more pleasurable than not using it, regardless of cost. Many addicts, probably a majority, resist and resent oral methadone maintenance because methadone, though it can prevent withdrawal pains, does not, when taken orally, supply them with the euphoric "high" they associate with heroin. (Intravenous use of methadone will produce a "high" comparable to that of heroin. The oral use of methadone is seen by addicts as a way to avoid the pain of heroin withdrawal but not as an alternative source of a "high.") Persons willingly on methadone tend to be older addicts who are "burned out," i.e., physically and mentally run down by the burdens of maintaining a heroin habit. A younger addict still enjoying his "run" (which may last five or ten years) will be less inclined to shift to methadone.

The "Contagion" Model

WHEN ASKED how they got started on heroin, addicts almost universally give the same answer: They were offered some by a friend. They tried it, often in a group setting, and they liked it. Although not every person who tries it will like it, and not every person who likes it will become addicted to it, a substantial fraction (perhaps a quarter) of first users become regular and heavy users. Heroin use spreads through peer-group contacts, and those peer groups most vulnerable to experimenting with it are those that include a person who himself has recently tried it and whose enthusiasm for it is contagious. In fact, so common is this process that many observers use the word "contagious" or "contagion" deliberately—the spread of heroin use is in the nature of an epidemic in which a "carrier" (a recent and enthusi-astic convert to heroin) "infects" a population with whom he is in close contact.

A study in Chicago revealed in some detail how this process of infection occurs. Patrick H. Hughes and Gail A. Crawford found that a major heroin "epidemic" occurred in Chicago after World War II, reached a peak in 1949, was followed by a decline in the number of new cases of addiction during the 1950s, with signs of a new epidemic appearing in the early 1960s.[4] They studied closely eleven neighborhood-sized epi-demics that they were able to identify in the late 1960s, each producing fifty or more new addicts. In the great majority of cases, not only was the new user turned on by a friend, but the friend was himself a novice user still exhilarated by the thrill of a "high." Both recruit and initiator tended to be members of a small group that had already experimented heavily with many drugs and with alcohol. These original friendship groups broke up as the heavy users formed new associations in order to main-tain their habits. Strikingly, the new user usually does not seek out heroin the first time he uses it, but rather begins to use it al-most fortuitously, by the accident of personal contact in a poly-drug subculture. A majority of the members of these groups usually try heroin after it is introduced by one of them, though not all of these become addicted.

Such a theory explains the very rapid rates of increase in a city such as Boston. The number of new users will be some ex-ponential function of the number of initial users. Obviously, this geometric growth rate would soon, if not checked by other factors, make addicts of us all. Since we are not all going to become addicts, other factors must be at work, though their na-ture is not well understood. They may include "natural immu-nity" (some of us may find heroin unpleasant), breaks in the chain of contagion (caused by the absence of any personal link-ages between peer groups using heroin and peer groups that are not), and the greater difficulty in some communities of finding a supply of heroin. Perhaps most important, the analogy between heroin use and disease is imperfect: We do not choose to contract smallpox from a friend, but we do choose to use heroin offered by a friend.

The Myth of the "Pusher"

IF HEROIN use is something we choose, then the moral and empirical judgments one makes about heroin become important. If a person thinks heroin use wrong, if he believes that heroin use can cause a serious pathology, then, other things being equal, he will be less likely to use it than if he made the opposite judgments. Chein found that the belief that heroin use was wrong was a major reason given by heroin "dabblers" for not continuing in its use. The extent to which belief in the wrongness of heroin use depends on its being illegal is unknown, but it is interesting to note that many addicts tend to be strongly opposed to legalizing heroin.

The peer-group/contagion model also helps explain why the fastest increase in heroin use has been among young people, with the result that the average age of known addicts has fallen sharply in the last few years. In Boston the Harvard student group found that one-quarter of heroin users seeking help from a public agency were under the age of eighteen, and 80 per cent were under twenty-five. A study done at American University found that the average age at which indentifiable addicts in Washington, D.C., began using heroin was under nineteen. Though stories of youngsters under fifteen becoming addicts are commonplace, most studies place the beginning of heavy use between the ages of seventeen and nineteen. It is persons in this age group, of course, who are most exposed to the contagion: They are intensely involved in peer groups; many have begun to become part of "street society" because they either dropped out of or graduated from schools; and they are most likely to suffer from boredom and a desire "to prove themselves." It is claimed that many of those who become serious addicts "mature out" of their heroin use sometime in their thirties, in much the same way that many juvenile delinquents spontaneously cease committing criminal acts when they get older. Unfortunately, not much is known about "maturing out," and it is even possible that it is a less common cause of ending heroin use than death or imprisonment.

If this view of the spread of addiction is correct, then it is pointless to explain heroin use as something that "pushers" inflict on unsuspecting youth. The popular conception of a stranger in a dirty trenchcoat hanging around schoolyards and corrupting innocent children is largely myth—indeed, given what we know about addiction, it would almost have to be myth. No dealer in drugs is likely to risk doing business with strangers. The chances of apprehension are too great and the profits from dealing with friends too substantial to make missionary work among unknown "straights" worthwhile. And the novice user is far more likely to take the advice of a friend, or to respond to the blandishments of a peer group, than to take an unfamiliar product from an anonymous pusher.

An important implication of the peer-group/contagion model is that programs designed to treat or control established addicts may have little effect on the mechanism whereby heroin use spreads. Users tend to be "infectious" only early in their heroin careers (later, all their friends are addicts and the life style seems less glamorous), and at this stage they are not likely to volunteer for treatment or to come to the attention of police authorities. In the Chicago study, for example, Hughes and Crawford found that police efforts directed at addiction were intensified only after the peak of the epidemic had passed, and though arrests increased sharply, they were principally of heavily addicted regular users, not infectious users. No matter whether one favors a medical or a law-enforcement approach to heroin, the optimum strategy depends crucially on whether one's objective is to "treat" existing addicts or to prevent the recruitment of new ones.

Crime and Heroin

THE AMOUNT of crime committed by addicts is no doubt large, but exactly how large is a matter of conjecture. And most important, the amount of addict crime undertaken solely to support the habit, and thus the amount by which crime would decrease if the price of heroin fell to zero, is unknown. Estimates of the proportion of all property crime committed by addicts range from 25 to 67 per cent. Whatever the true fraction, there is no reason to assume that property crimes would decline by that fraction if heroin became free. Some addicts are criminals before they are addicts and would remain criminals if their addiction, like their air and water, cost them virtually nothing. Furthermore, some addicts who steal to support their habit come to regard crime as more profitable than normal employment. They would probably continue to steal to provide themselves with an income even after they no longer needed to use part of that income to buy heroin.

Just as it is wrong to suppose that an unwitting youth has heroin "pushed" on him, so also it is wrong to suppose that these youth only then turn to crime to support their habit. Various studies of known addicts have shown that between half and three-quarters were known to be delinquent before turning to drugs. In a random sample of adult black males studied in St. Louis (14 per cent of whom turned out to have records for using or selling narcotics), 60 per cent of those who tried heroin and 73 per cent of those who became addicted to it had previously acquired a police record. Put another way, one-quarter of the delinquents, but only 4 per cent of the nondelinquents, became heroin addicts.[5]

That addicts are recruited disproportionately from the ranks of those who already have a criminal history may be a relatively recent phenomenon. The history of heroin use in New York City compiled by Edward Preble and John J. Casey, Jr., suggests that in the period before 1951 heroin use grew slowly and often occurred through "snorting" (inhaling the powder) rather than "mainlining" (injecting liquefied heroin into a vein).[6] The heroin used was of high quality and low cost, and its consumption took place in social settings in which many users were not criminals but rather entertainers, musicians, and so on. The heroin epidemic that began around 1951 was caused by the new popularity of the drug among younger people on the streets, especially street gang members looking for a new "high." (Indeed, one theory of the breakup of those gangs romanticized in *West Side Story* is that heroin use became a status symbol, such that the young man "nodding" on the corner or hustling and dealing in dope became the figure to be emulated, rather than the fighter and the leader of gang wars. A group of heavy addicts, each of whom is preoccupied with his own "high," will soon find collective action—and thus gang life—all but impossible.) Mainlining became commonplace, increased demand led to a rise in price and decline in quality of the available heroin, and the level of heroin-connected crime increased.

Some supportive evidence for the increase in recruitment of addicts from among the ranks of the criminal is found in a study of white male Kentucky addicts done by John A. O'Donnell.[7] He traced the careers of two hundred sixty-six such persons who had been admitted to the U. S. Public Health Service Hospital in Lexington from its opening in 1935. The earlier the year and the younger the age in which the person first became addicted, the more likely he was to have committed criminal acts before addiction. The proportion of addicts with criminal records, and perhaps the rate of increase of those with such records, would probably be greater among a more typical population of addicts—for example, among urban blacks.

Once addicted, however, persons are likely to commit more

crimes than they would have had they not become addicted. The common and tragic testimony of street addicts dwells upon their need to find the money with which to support the habit, and this means for many of them "hustling," stealing heroin from other users, dealing in heroin themselves, or simply begging. The O'Donnell study in Kentucky provides statistical support for this view, though no estimate of the amount by which crime increases as a result of addiction.

The kinds of crimes committed by addicts are fairly well known. Selling heroin is perhaps the most important of these—the Hudson Institute estimated that almost half of the annual heroin consumption in New York is financed by selling heroin and related services (for example, selling or renting the equipment needed for injecting heroin). Of the nondrug crimes, shoplifting, burglary, and prostitution account for the largest proportion of addict income used for drug purchases—perhaps 40 to 50 per cent.[8] Though the addict wants money, he will not confine himself to those crimes in which property is taken with no threat to personal safety. Muggings and armed robberies will be committed regularly by some addicts, and occasionally by many; even in a burglary, violence may result if the addict is surprised by the victim while ransacking the latter's home or store.

The amount of property taken by addicts is large, but probably not as large as some of the more popular estimates would have us believe. Max Singer has shown that those who make these estimates—usually running into the billions of dollars per year in New York City alone—fail to reconcile their figures with the total amount of property known or suspected to be stolen. He estimated that no more than $500 million a year is lost to both addicted and nonaddicted burglars, shoplifters, pickpockets, robbers, and assorted thieves in New York. If all of that were taken by addicts (which of course it isn't) and if there were one hundred thousand addicts in the city, then the average addict would be stealing about $5,000 worth of goods a year—not a vast sum. Even the more conservative figure of sixty thousand addicts would raise the maximum average theft loss per addict to only $8,000.[9]

Despite the fact that many addicts were criminals before addiction and would remain criminals even if they ended their addiction, and despite the fact that the theft losses to addicts are considerably exaggerated, there is little doubt that addiction produces a significant increase in criminality of two kinds—stealing from innocent victims and selling heroin illegally to willing consumers. More accurately, the heroin black market provides incentives for at least two kinds of antisocial acts—theft (with its attendant fear) and spreading the use of heroin further.

Heroin and Law Enforcement

CRITICS of the "punitive" mode of attacking heroin distribution argue that law enforcement has not only failed to protect society against these social costs, it has increased those costs by driving up the price of heroin and thus the amount of criminality necessary to support heroin habits. If by this they mean that law enforcement has "failed" because it has not reduced the heroin traffic to zero—and anything short of this will increase the price of heroin—then of course the statement is true. It would be equally true, and equally misleading, to say that most medical approaches have "failed" because the vast majority of persons who undergo voluntary treatment at Lexington or other hospitals return to heroin use when they are released.

Apart from methadone maintenance, which deserves separate discussion, existing therapeutic methods for treating heroin addiction are extremely expensive and have low success rates. Various investigators have found a relapse rate for addicts discharged from hospitals after having undergone treatment ranging between 90 and 95 per cent. Over time, a certain fraction of those treated will begin to become permanently abstinent—Dr.

George Vaillant estimates it at about 2 per cent a year—but most of those do not do so voluntarily.[10] The Kentucky males studied by O'Donnell displayed relatively high rates of abstinence after release from the hospital, but this was due mostly to the fact that heroin itself became more or less unavailable in Kentucky. The New York addicts studied by Vaillant who had been released from the same hospital showed much lower rates of abstinence, in part because heroin was easy to find in New York; those who did abstain tended to be those placed under some form of compulsory community supervision, such as intensive parole. And even these did not become entirely "clean"—typically they found a substitute for heroin and most often became alcoholics.

The fact that medical approaches do not "cure" addiction, especially if the addict must volunteer for them, need not trouble the critics of the law-enforcement approach if they believe that only the tangible social cost of addiction (e.g., crime) and not addiction itself is a problem, or if they concede that addiction is a problem but think it wrong for addicts to be compelled to obtain help.

But if law enforcement at present fails to prevent the "external" costs of addiction (i.e., crime), or even increases those costs, this will also remain true under any likely alternative public policy, unless one is willing to support complete legalization of heroin for all who wish it. Yet no advocate of "decriminalizing" heroin with whom I am familiar supports total legalization. Most favor some version of the British system, by which heroin is dispensed at low cost in government-controlled clinics to known addicts in order to maintain them in their habit. Almost no one seems to favor allowing any drugstore to sell, or any doctor to prescribe, heroin to anybody who wants it.

The reason for this reluctance is rarely made explicit. Presumably it is either political expediency (designed to make the British system more palatable to a skeptical American public) or an unspoken moral reservation about the desirability of heroin use per se, apart from its tangible social cost. I suspect that the chief reason is the latter: One's moral sensibilities are indeed shocked by the prospect of young children buying heroin at the drugstore the same way they now buy candy. And if one finds that scene wrong or distasteful, then one should also find the prospect of an adult nonuser having cheap access to heroin wrong or distasteful, unless one is willing to make a radical (and on medical grounds, hard to defend) distinction between what is good for a person under the age of (say) eighteen and what is good for a person over that age.

The total decriminalization of heroin would lead, all evidence suggests, to a sharp increase in its use. Indeed, precisely because of such an increase, the British in 1968 abandoned the practice of allowing physicians to prescribe heroin to anyone they wished.

The British System

UNDER post-1968 British policy, the sale of heroin to nonusers or to novice users is illegal. In clinics authorized to prescribe heroin, the doctor must not do so unless he is certain the patient is addicted and truly needs the drug, and he should then prescribe conservatively. The aim is to maintain the patient with enough heroin to be free of withdrawal pains, but not enough so that he will have any surplus to sell or give to others.

The result is that a black market in heroin still exists in Britain. As Griffith Edwards (of the Addiction Research Unit, Institute of Psychiatry, London) has pointed out, the British system "in fact cuts down but in no way eliminates the potential population of black-market customers." [11] That market, the size of which is unknown but in his view is not negligible, is made up of "customers" of the clinic system who want larger doses in order to get a "high," addicts who for various reasons do not wish to register with the government, and would-be novice users who would like to try heroin.

If this is a problem in Britain, which has only two thousand or so addicts, it would be a much greater problem in the United States, where there are one or two hundred times as many addicts, a large fraction of whom are quite young. Those willing to be maintained on low dosages in a government clinic are probably those who fear withdrawal pains more than they cherish the heroin "high"; in short, they are likely to be addicts who have passed beyond the stage of missionary zeal about an exciting new thrill. They may be similar to those addicts in the United States who volunteer for methadone maintenance. (This is all supposition, for I know of no detailed comparative studies of British and American addicts. I think it a reasonable supposition, however.) It is possible, in short, that the number of addict-zealots in the United States would be large enough to continue the spread of heroin to new users and to maintain an active black market, even if the United States were to adopt some version of the British clinic method.

It is important to bear in mind that the residual black market need not be large in order to supply novice users and thus continue the infection-recruitment process. Even if the vast majority of confirmed addicts registered to receive government heroin (which is unlikely, unless the government were willing to supply euphoria-producing rather than simply maintenance doses), the increase in the number of new addicts among susceptible groups could continue to be quite rapid and to be supplied out of a black market of modest proportions.

Furthermore, there is some reason to believe that British and American addicts are sufficiently different so that an American clinic system would not attract as large a proportion of the total addict population as have the British clinics. A member of the Addiction Research Institute in London is quoted by Edgar May as observing that the typical British addict is likely to be a "middle-class drop-out" rather than a lower-class "oblivion-seeker." [12] The contemporary British addict, in short, may be more similar to the American addict before 1920 (when the use of opiates was increasing in the middle classes) than to the

143

American addict of today. The difference, if correct, may have profound consequences for the efficacy of control techniques. The use of opiates among middle-class Americans dropped sharply after they were made illegal and law enforcement got underway, just as the use of heroin by the British has apparently stabilized since heroin was made illegal except through licensed clinics.

This possibility is worth bearing in mind when we interpret accounts of the British system. The success of the plan (that is, the apparent stabilization in the number of addicts and the absence of addict-related crime) is in part the result of imposing on a middle-class addict population stricter controls than had once existed—and doing so after the rather easy availability of heroin had resulted in a *fortyfold increase* in the number of known addicts during the preceding fifteen years. If the size of the American addict population grew rapidly when possession of heroin was already illegal, it is a bit hard to understand what there is in either the British experience or our own that would lead one to conclude that the number of addicts here would be stabilized or reduced if heroin were made easier to get. At best, decriminalization would reduce somewhat the size of the black market (while simultaneously lowering prices in that market) and reduce by an unknown but probably significant fraction the amount of crime committed by those addicts willing to avail themselves of the maintenance doses to be obtained at government clinics.

The Effectiveness of Law Enforcement

UNDER ANY conceivable American variant of the British system, then, a law-enforcement strategy would remain an important component of government policy. Rather than simply rejecting law enforcement as "punitive" (and therefore "medieval," "barbarian," "counterproductive," or whatever), one ought to consider what it might accomplish under various circumstances.

The assumption that law enforcement has no influence on the size of the addict population but does have an effect on the price of heroin (and thus on crime committed to meet that higher price) rests chiefly on the evidence that the majority of known addicts have been arrested at least once; that during his life expectancy, any addict is virtually certain to be arrested; and that, despite this, the addict returns to his habit and to the criminal life needed to sustain it. These facts are essentially correct. The difficulty lies in equating "law enforcement" with "arrest."

Thousands of addicts are arrested every year; a very large proportion are simply returned to the street—by the police, who wish to use them as informants, or by judges who wish to place them on probation or under suspended sentences because they believe (rightly) that a prison term will not cause their cure or rehabilitation. Only a few addicts are singled out for very severe punishment. We do not know for how many addicts arrest is simply a revolving door. In Boston, however, Wheat has done a careful study of the relationship between the level of law enforcement, defined as the "expected costs" of an arrest to the user, and the number of addicts in the city. By "expected costs," Wheat means the probability of being arrested multiplied by the probability of being sentenced to prison and the length of the average prison sentence. Though his numerical estimates are complex and open to criticism, the general relationship between the number of heroin users and the expected "costs" to the addict of law enforcement is quite striking—the "costs" declined sharply between 1961 and 1970, while the estimated number of addicts in Boston increased about tenfold. Furthermore, the largest increases in the number of addicts tended to follow years in which the certainty and severity of law enforcement were the lowest.[13]

More specifically: (1) From 1961 to 1965, the estimated proportion of users arrested by the police declined (it started to increase again in 1966); (2) the chances that an arrested user would be sentenced to jail declined from better than one in two in 1960 to only one in ten in 1970; and (3) the length of the average sentence imposed fell from about twenty-three months in 1961 to fewer than fifteen months in 1969, though there were some intervening ups and downs. By 1970, the chance of a heroin addict being sent to jail during any given year was rather remote. We do not know whether similar changes occurred in other cities, though given the cause of the changes—the growing (and erroneous) view among legislators and judges that addicts should be referred to psychiatrists for (nonexistent) "help"—we suspect that many cities, influenced by the same sentiments, may have experienced the same changes. In Chicago, for example, Hughes and his colleagues have shown that the number of arrests of addicts, and the average sentence given to those convicted, rose dramatically during or just after the heroin epidemic of 1947–1950, but by 1955 the length of sentence had begun to fall again, and by 1960 it was almost down to the prewar level.[14]

If there is a relationship between law enforcement and heroin use, it may result from one or both of two processes. An increase in legal penalties may deter the novice user from further use or it may deter the confirmed addict-dealer (or if he is jailed, prevent him entirely) from selling to a potential user. Lessening the "costs" of the penalty may either embolden the novice users and potential users, or improve their access to a supplier, or both.

There is some clinical evidence that both processes are in fact at work. Robert Schasre's study of forty Mexican-American heroin users who had stopped shooting heroin revealed that over half (twenty-two) did so involuntarily after they had lost their source of supply—their dealer had been arrested or had lost his source, or the user himself had moved to another community where he could find no dealer. Of the remaining eighteen who stopped "voluntarily," most did so in response to some social or institutional pressure; in a third of these cases, that pressure was having been arrested or having a friend who was arrested on a narcotics charge.[15]

Indeed, one could as easily make the argument that law enforcement has not even been tried as the argument that it has been tried and failed. Before making it, please be reassured that such an argument does not bespeak an illusion that prison sentences "cure" addiction nor indicate a desire to "seek vengeance" on the addict. The same argument could be made if one substituted for "sentences to prison," sentences to Synanon, Daytop, methadone maintenance, or expensive psychiatric clinics. The central point is that only a small proportion of heroin addicts will voluntarily seek and remain in any form of treatment, care, or confinement—unless that care involves free dispensation of heroin itself.

One can imagine a variety of law-enforcement strategies that would have a powerful effect on the number of addicts on the street, and thus on the number of street crimes they might commit and other harm they might do to others and themselves. One could arrest every known addict and send him to a "heroin quarantine center" with comfortable accommodations and intensive care programs. Or one could arrest every known addict and send him back onto the street under a "pledge" system requiring him to submit to frequent urine tests which, if omitted or failed, would then lead to confinement in either center or jail.

American society does not do these things for a number of reasons. One is that, despite popular talk, we do not really take the problem that seriously—or at least have not until white middle-class suburbanites began to suffer from a problem only ghetto blacks once endured. Another is that we think that detaining addicts for the mere fact of addiction is violative of their civil rights. (It is an interesting question. We quarantine people with smallpox without thinking that their rights are violated. The similarities as well as the differences are worth some public debate.) Finally, we do not do these things because we labor under the misapprehension that law enforcement should concentrate on the "pushers" and the "big connections" and not on the innocent user.

The last reason may be the weakest of all, even if among tough-sounding politicians it is the most common. In the first place, the "pusher" is largely a myth, or more accurately, he is simply the addict playing one of his roles. And the "big connections" and "top dealers," who indeed exist and who generally are not users, are in many ways the least important part of the heroin market system—because they are the most easily replaced. A new "connection" arises for every one put out of business. The amount of heroin seized by federal agents is only a fraction of what is imported.

This last fact has led many persons in and out of government to speak critically of the Administration's effort to eliminate the legal growing of opium poppies in Turkey. There is not much doubt that in time the present American heroin market could be supplied by alternative, and harder to control, poppy fields in Southeast Asia and elsewhere. One study suggests that the entire estimated American consumption of heroin would require fewer than ten square miles of poppy fields. There may be compelling political reasons, however, for pressing the crop eradication program. It is hard to imagine a president launching a serious effort to constrain heroin users or heroin dealers if he were to ignore the foreign manufacture and importation of heroin. Indeed, he would run the risk of being accused not only of ignoring foreign producers, but perhaps even of actively helping them wage what some would no doubt call "chemical warfare" against America's ghetto poor. Some such criticisms are forthcoming despite the crop eradication program; witness the charge by a Yale scholar that the Central Intelligence Agency was assisting heroin traffickers in Southeast Asia. Witness also the outrage of Congressman Charles Rangel from Harlem at the prospect that the Turks intend to resume poppy cultivation.

Furthermore, elimination of the Turkish poppy crop was in fact associated with a sharp decline in the amount of illicit morphine base moving through the trafficking networks of Europe. Intelligence reports from various European cities indicated that heroin manufacturers were experiencing great difficulty in acquiring their raw materials. This shortage was accompanied by intense French police pressure on the illegal heroin laboratories in the Marseilles area, with several major arrests, seizure of much equipment, and (in one case) confiscation of a half ton of finished heroin secreted in the hull of a fishing boat.

These factors contributed, at least in the short run, to a marked shortage of heroin at the retail level on the streets of our large Eastern cities. Prices rose and quality decreased sharply. By 1973 the price of a bag of heroin had doubled over what it was in the late 1960s, and what one could purchase for the new, higher price was often no more than 2 or 3 per cent pure—so weak that regular users of it could often be rather easily detoxified.

At the same time, heroin usage was declining. All the measures used to estimate heroin consumption were down or had leveled off—the number of heroin overdose deaths, the percentage of arrested persons in Washington, D.C., found to have heroin traces in their urine, the rate of serum hepatitus, and the number of persons seeking admission to methadone clinics.

This drop in heroin use, which by 1974 was widely reported by a number of independent sources, cannot be ascribed entirely to law-enforcement pressure or to treatment programs. There had been a substantial element of fad and novelty in the heroin experimentation in the 1960s. The havoc wreaked on the lives of young persons was readily seen by the next generation, and many decided that what once was thought fun was in fact a catastrophe. Many militant black leaders began associating drugs with the oppression of the white community, thereby providing their followers with ideological as well as personal reasons for staying clean. Many poor and working-class blacks, terrified of the addict, began supporting punitive countermeasures. But law enforcement and the availability of a variety of treatment programs surely played a role in this decline. The former literally priced heroin out of the market for many users, while the latter provided an alternative way of coping with their drug dependence. As a result, though the scarcity of heroin from France and Turkey was partially offset by the increased importation of heroin manufactured in Mexico and Southeast Asia, consumption on the East Coast did not, so far as one can tell, return to its previous level.

To understand why that happened, one must consider the heroin delivery system at the street level and how it reacts to changes in price and demand.

Containing the Contagion

THE NOVICE or would-be heroin user is quite vulnerable to changes, even small ones, in the availability of heroin. For one thing, a person who has not yet become a heavy user will not conduct an intensive search for a supply. Some studies have suggested that a "dabbler" may use heroin if it is immediately available, but will not use it if it requires two, three, or four hours of searching. Extending the search time for novices may discourage or reduce the frequency of their use of heroin. In addition, a dealer is reluctant to sell to persons with whom he is not closely acquainted for fear of detection and apprehension by the police. When police surveillance is intensified, the dealer becomes more cautious about those with whom he does business. A casual user or distant acquaintance represents a threat to the dealer when police activity is high; when such activity is low, the casual or new customer is more attractive. Heroin customers can be thought of as a "queue" with the heaviest users at the head of the line and the casual ones at the end; how far down the queue the dealer will do business depends on the perceived level of risk associated with each additional customer, and that in turn depends on how strongly "the heat is on."

The price of heroin to the user will be affected by law enforcement in different ways, depending on the focus of the pressure. No one has the data with which to construct anything but a highly conjectural model of the heroin market; at the same time, there is little reason for asserting that the only effect of law enforcement on the heroin market is to drive up the price of the product.

Enforcement aimed at the sources of supply may well drive up the price. The price of a "bag" on the street has risen steeply since the early 1950s, and simultaneously the quality of the product has declined (which means that the real price increase is even higher than the nominal one). This was the result of a vast increase in demand (the heroin "epidemic" of the 1950s and 1960s) coupled with the increase in risks associated with dealing in the product. The long-term effect of law-enforcement pressures on large-scale dealers is probably to force up the price of heroin by either increasing the cash price, decreasing the quality of the product, or requiring dealers to discriminate among their customers in order to avoid risky sales. But in the short term, antidealer law enforcement probably affects access (finding a "connection") more than price.

Suppose that law enforcement were directed at the user and the street-level dealer rather than the top supplier. Taking user-dealers off the streets in large numbers would tend to reduce the demand for, and thus the price of, heroin. Furthermore, with many heavy customers gone, some dealers would have to accept the risks of doing business with novice users who, having smaller habits or no real habits at all, would consume fewer bags per capita and pay lower prices. (Law enforcement aimed merely at known and regular users would not result in the apprehension of many novice users, however, and thus would not take off the streets a large fraction of the sources of heroin "infection.") Suppose, finally, that coupled with law enforcement aimed at known user-dealers there were a selective strategy of identifying and restraining the agents of contagion. This was tried in Chicago on an experimental basis by Hughes and Crawford, with promising though not conclusive results. On spotting a neighborhood epidemic, they intervened by seeking quickly to identify the friends and fellow users of an addict. They found in this case that one addict led them to fourteen other addicts and, most important, to seven persons experimenting with heroin. The doctors were able to involve eleven of the fourteen addicts and five of the seven experimenters in a treatment program; the remainder of the experimenters apparently discontinued heroin use, perhaps because the social structure in which their drug use took place was disrupted.[16]

There is, of course, an alternative way to get many confirmed addicts out of the heroin black market, and that is to offer them heroin legally at nominal prices. A black market would still exist for novice users, unregistered regular users, and registered regular users who wish to supplement their government-supplied maintenance dose with an additional dose that would produce a "high." Furthermore, this black market would be in many ways more attractive to the euphoria-seeking user because, due to competition from government suppliers, prices in it would be lower than the price in the existing market. Under this system, the government-maintained users would remain on the street and some fraction of them would continue to serve as contagion agents, thus causing the size of the addict population to continue to grow. Whether it would grow as fast as it has in the past, no one can say. There is little evidence of any rapid growth in England, but as pointed out above, this may be due to the fact that British addicts are different from American ones and the illegal supply of heroin is much smaller there than it is here. Indeed, any estimate of the future size of the addict population under any set of legal constraints is almost meaningless. We simply do not know how many persons are susceptible to heroin use if exposed to it nor what fraction of the population that is at risk is now using heroin.

Methadone Maintenance

METHADONE is an addictive synthetic opiate that has become the basis of the single most important heroin treatment program in the United States. Although methadone itself is addictive (after regular use, withdrawal produces pain), it has advantages over heroin: It may be taken orally; it produces no "high" if used orally; in large doses it seems to "block" the euphoric effect of heroin and prevent the craving for heroin; its effects last for about twenty-four hours (as opposed to about six hours for heroin); and it has no significant harmful side effects. If methadone is injected (as is often the case in Britain), it can produce a "high" and a risk of a harmful overdose. And if taken orally in small dosages, methadone will not block the high that results from injecting heroin, though it may continue to suppress the craving for heroin. Because it will produce a "high" when injected, a black market in methadone has developed and deaths from overdosage have been reported.

There are a number of controversies about the proper use of methadone and indeed about the ethics of using it at all. Doctors disagree over whether the addict should get the large "blockage" dose or only the small "anticraving" dose, over whether the methadone patient should be required to accept various ancillary services (e.g., psychiatric help, job counseling), and over whether efforts can or should be made to withdraw the patient from methadone. Others argue over the morality of feeding an addiction and, inevitably, running the risk of addicting some persons who were not addicted when they entered the program. For this reason, most methadone clinics screen candidates carefully to insure that only confirmed heroin users are admitted; this means that young persons tend to be excluded.

Evaluations that have been made so far of methadone generally term it a success. By "success" is meant that the patients tend to stay in the program, those who stay in the program tend to become employable, and those who stay in the program do not return to regular use of heroin (though some may experiment with it from time to time). The evidence as to whether persons on methadone abstain from criminality is not as clear. Dr. Frances Gearing of Columbia University, who headed the largest evaluation program, found that the number of arrests and incarcerations of persons who entered a methadone program fell dramatically.[17] A study in the Bedford-Stuyvesant area of Brooklyn, on the other hand, found some evidence that many successful methadone patients remain employed in criminal occupations (e.g., shoplifters, prostitutes), not only because that is the only trade they know, but also because, once they are freed of the need for heroin, that trade becomes even more profitable than before.[18]

The central problem with methadone maintenance, however, is beyond dispute. So long as it remains a voluntary program, methadone is only attractive to those addicts who are tired of the life style of the addict, who no longer cherish the heroin "high" to the exclusion of all else, and who are otherwise "burned out." It is for this reason that the average methadone patient is between thirty and thirty-five years of age, while the average heroin addict is much younger. The typical methadone patient has been a heroin addict for ten to fifteen years and now finds methadone a more attractive choice than heroin. This means that the number of addicts who can be helped by a voluntary methadone program may be no more than one-third or one-half of the total addict population. And most important, it means that voluntary methadone maintenance holds little attraction for the kind of addict who is a contagion agent—young, excited by the heroin "high," and eager to convert his "straight" friends to its use.

Other forms of chemical treatment may be developed for heroin addiction. "Antagonists"—drugs that prevent subsequently injected opiates from having any effect and that produce painful withdrawal symptoms in persons who have previously injected heroin—exist, but either have undesirable side effects or are not long-acting. Furthermore, since they do not produce a "high," and in addition do not reduce the craving for heroin, relatively few addicts are likely to volunteer for their use.

Possible Policy Directions

IF NOTHING else, this discussion of the complexities of heroin use, marketing, and control should suggest the futility of arguments between the so-called "punitive" and "medical" approaches to addiction, the simplistic nature of unqualified recommendations that we adopt the "British system," and the imprecision of angry disputes between those who wish to "get tough" on "pushers" and those who wish to "decriminalize" heroin.

Beyond that, thinking about heroin requires one first of all to decide how one will handle the underlying philosophical issue—namely, whether the state is ever justified in protecting people from themselves, or whether it can only intervene to protect an innocent party from the actions of someone else. Put another way, the question is whether the state has any responsibility for the quality of human life in those cases where that quality (or lack of it) appears to be the result of freely exercised choice with no external effects on other parties. It is my view that the state does have such responsibilities, though its powers in this regard must be carefully exercised toward only the most important and reasonable goals. Even John Stuart Mill, whose defense of personal liberty is virtually absolute, argued against allowing a man to sell himself into slavery, "for by selling himself as a slave, he abdicates his liberty; he foregoes any future use of it beyond that simple act."

The next question is whether heroin addiction is such a form of "slavery" or is otherwise a state of being which should not be left to free choice. This is a more difficult question to answer in general terms, for somewhat surprisingly, we know rather little about what proportion of all heroin users are seriously incapacitated (or "captured") by it. Obviously, a large number are; but some might remain heavy users and yet hold jobs, lead responsible family lives, and retain other attributes of their humanity. Nobody knows what fraction are in this category, though we do know that the advocates of decriminalization tend to give (with little or no evidence) very generous estimates of it, while proponents of "stamping out" heroin give very small ones. The lives of British addicts have not been carefully studied. But Griffith Edwards of the Addiction Research Institute reports "the impression of many of the clinic doctors" that "the majority of young heroin takers do not settle to a job, or otherwise manage their lives responsibly, do not keep to the prescribed dose, and tend to acquire drugs other than those prescribed." [19] Furthermore, the mortality rate of British addicts, even without the need to steal to support a habit, is twenty-eight times as large as the death rate for the equivalent age group in the British population and twice that of American heroin addicts. [20]

I think it clear that for a sufficiently large number of persons, heroin is so destructive of the human personality that it should not be made generally available. (Defending that view in the context of the current debate is not essential, however, because not even the most zealous advocate of decriminalization supports complete legalization.) I believe this to be the case, though I recognize the rejoinders that can be made. Alcohol, some will say, has consequences for many individuals and for society at least as destructive as those of heroin, yet no one would propose returning to a system of prohibition. Alcohol and heroin are different problems, however, both medically and legally. A far smaller proportion of alcohol users than of heroin users become addicted in any meaningful sense of that term; the risks to the average individual of experimentation are accordingly far less in the former than in the latter case. And of those "addicted" to alcohol, there have been a larger proportion of "cures," although perhaps not as many as one would wish. Finally, alcohol use is so widespread as to be nearly universal, while heroin use remains an exotic habit of relatively few, and thus presents easier problems of control. Perhaps because of this, while no advanced society has been able to eliminate alcohol use, most societies have been able to eliminate, or keep to trifling proportions, heroin use.

If one accepts the view that it is desirable and possible, not only to provide better treatment for present addicts, but to reduce the rate of growth of the addict population, then one must also accept the need for some measure of compulsion; nothing is clearer than the fact that most young addicts enjoying their "run" will not voluntarily choose a life without heroin in preference to a life with it. Such compulsion will be necessary whatever disposition is made of the constrained addict—whether he be put on probation or sent to prison, to a quarantine center, to a methadone program, or to a heroin maintenance program. The compulsion will be necessary to achieve two objectives: to insure that he remains in the appropriate treatment without "cheating" (i.e., simply using the treatment center as a cheap source of drugs to be sold on the street), and to insure that while treated he does not proselytize among nonaddicts and spread the contagion. Furthermore, there is some evidence (inconclusive, to be sure) that the possibility of arrest followed by some penalty deters at least some potential users and makes access to heroin more difficult for others.

Finally, to the extent that people voluntarily elect not to use heroin, the fact of its illegality may contribute to the belief that such use is "wrong," and therefore enhance the probability that a nonuser will remain a nonuser. Or put another way, it is difficult to see how society can assert that heroin use is a grave evil if it also must admit that its use is perfectly legal.

A detailed consideration of the legal policies which might

most effectively deal with the heroin problem is beyond the scope of this chapter. In general, there are two alternatives—"outpatient" programs (in which the addict is left in the community but under a legally enforced requirement to report periodically for tests and for chemical or other forms of treatment) and "inpatient" programs (in which the addict is separated from the community in detoxification, methadone, or other programs). Each kind of program must deal with both regular addicts and infectious, novice addicts. The legal, medical, and organizational issues involved in these alternatives are complex. The important thing, however, is to consider them seriously—which means in turn to stop thinking of "legal" and "medical" approaches as mutually exclusive or separately viable.

Perhaps the most difficult of these issues is to decide what role heroin maintenance itself can play in an overall addict control program. It seems likely that offering low-cost, high-quality heroin is the one positive inducement that will prove attractive to most young addicts still enjoying their "run." Under the British system, the addict who obtains heroin from clinics is under no other obligations; no doctor or government official has the power to compel (and some doctors do not even have the desire to ask) the addict to accept, as a condition of heroin maintenance, any form of therapy, including the gradual substitution of oral methadone for heroin. In the British context, with a tiny addict population composed of persons apparently quite different from the typical American addict, that policy may work well enough, though experience with it is still too short to permit one to be confident of its value.

But whatever the fate of the British experiment, it seems probable that any larger program will involve real risks of sustaining the habits of contagion agents likely to recruit new addicts, and of supplying, through illegal diversions, the existing black market in drugs. With the best will in the world, it is probably impossible to devise a government program run by ordinary mortals that can provide heroin to one or two hundred thousand addicts on an outpatient basis in a way that will avoid subsidizing the growth of the addict pool and supplying debilitating (as opposed to mere maintenance) doses. If that is true, and if our society believes that it has some responsibility for preventing addiction, then a substantial measure of legal compulsion will have to accompany any treatment program, especially one involving heroin maintenance.

Polydrug Abuse

THE APPARENT decline in some cities in heroin consumption in 1973 and 1974, coupled with the emergence of excess capacity in many treatment programs, has shifted attention away from heroin to so-called "polydrug" abuse—the abuse, that is, of a wide variety of chemical substances, including amphetamines, barbiturates, and hypnotics. For simplicity's sake, it might be thought of as the "pill problem." Of course, the pill problem has always existed side-by-side with heroin addiction, but with less attention because of the popular horror associated with heroin and its presumed connection with increased criminality. In fact, some pills can be as dangerous as heroin. Certain barbiturates, for example, are addictive, and unsupervised efforts to withdraw from their use can cause death.

We know rather little about the number or kind of people who so abuse pills that they can be said to constitute a public problem, as opposed to a private one involving themselves, their families, and their physician. It does not help to cite statistics about the number of housewives who take amphetamines to lose weight or the number of businessmen who take barbiturates in order to sleep. These practices may be unwise, even to a degree harmful, but they are not clearly so destructive of the personality or bound up with the recruitment of others into a drug culture that they are offensive to public decency or a threat to the life of the community.

Some heroin addicts use pills either in conjunction with heroin or as a temporary substitute when it is unavailable. Peer groups in which heroin use has developed tend to have also experimented with almost every other chemical imaginable. A dramatic example of the role of pills was provided by American servicemen returning from Southeast Asia. A careful study by Dr. Lee Robbins, under Defense Department sponsorship, revealed that a large fraction—over 40 per cent—of the enlisted men in the sample had used heroin while in Vietnam or adjoining areas, but that a year after their return to the United States scarcely any were still using it. (It seems likely that one reason so few became permanently addicted is that almost all inhaled or smoked the heroin and did not inject it.) Although very few heroin addicts were discovered among the veterans, the rate of abuse of alcohol and pills was quite high.[21]

Scarcely anybody is yet confident of what the proper public policy should be toward the polydrug problem. It seems clear that we can help reduce the rate of heroin consumption and help a significant fraction of addicts. It also seems clear that many who take pills, even to excess, are not engaging in behavior that should warrant our doing much more than urging them to seek competent medical advice. And it may be, for others who have no need for pills and who use them solely because of their ready availability among friends, that it is important for the government to tighten controls on production, distribution, and dispensation so as to keep harmful products out of the hands of the unwary or immature experimenter. But there is a certain small fraction of the population, regrettably large in absolute numbers, whose lives are in such disarray that drug dependence is a constant feature of their existence. The question is not whether they will take drugs, but only which and in what combinations. They may prefer heroin, but if it is unavailable they will instead steal methadone, try to obtain cocaine, or buy liquor and barbiturates. They are more to be pitied than to be feared, and we are as yet helpless to do very much for very many of them. We have not learned how to reach deeply into the lives of such persons; we can alter prices, change penalties, and provide counseling, but we cannot create character or restore a lost, or perhaps never extant, sense of identity.

Chapter 8

Courts and Corrections

MOST of the persons arrested for a serious crime have been arrested before. Indeed, one recent study estimates that over 87 per cent of those arrested will have been previously arrested—or, put a bit differently, the probability of being re-arrested is 0.87 chances in one, or close to a certainty.[1] The research by Marvin Wolfgang and his colleagues on ten thousand Philadelphia boys born in 1945 who lived in that city until they were at least eighteen years of age showed that, once a juvenile had been arrested three times, the chances of his being rearrested were over 70 per cent.[2] In their inquiry into New York City subway crimes, Jan M. Chaiken and his group at the Rand Institute conclude that, though there are hundreds of rob-beries on the subways each year, there could not be in the en-tire city of eight million more than *ten* persons who commit such robberies regularly and who have not been arrested at least once.[3]

No doubt for some persons—indeed, probably for most of us—the shame and burdens of arrest, even if no penalty follows, are a powerful deterrent. But the rearrest rates suggest that for others the mere fact of arrest is little or no deterrent. For such persons, who may commit the majority of all serious predatory crimes, the police are but a processing agency, inducting these arrestees once again into the familiar ritual of booking, making bail, arraignment, and pleading. Or as many police officers like to put it, "We operate the revolving door."

As crime became a popular and eventually a political issue, more attention was devoted to the police than to any other part of the criminal justice system. The frequency with which perpetrators of predatory crime are rearrested, however, should have alerted us to the possibility that, though the police need improvement, they are not the crucial agency in the system. Of far greater importance are those agencies that handle persons once arrested and that determine whether, how soon, and under what conditions they will be returned to the communities from which they came. These agencies are the criminal courts and the correctional institutions.

In theory, the function of the courts is to determine the guilt or innocence of the accused. In fact, it is to decide what to do with persons whose guilt or innocence is not at issue. Our judiciary is organized around the assumption that its theoretical function is its actual one—hence the emphasis on the adversary system, the rules of evidence, and the procedures and standards for testimony. In some jurisdictions, especially small ones with relatively few cases, the courts indeed act as theory would have it, and in all jurisdictions, even the big and busy ones, the courts will act that way some of the time. But most of the time, for most of the cases in our busier courts, the important decision concerns the sentence, not conviction or acquittal. In Manhattan, for example, only 3 per cent of the 13,555 persons indicted between July 1963 and July 1966 were convicted after a trial; almost 80 per cent pleaded guilty.[4] Even in one middle-sized, nonmetropolitan county in Wisconsin, 94 per cent of the convictions were the result of a plea of guilty, and it made little difference whether the offender had a lawyer or not.[5]

Everyone involved in the criminal justice system knows this, and increasingly the public at large is aware of it—or at least is aware that Perry Mason-style courtroom drama is found only on television, not in courtrooms. But despite this knowledge, very little has been done to equip the courts to perform their essential function well. Indeed, there has been very little serious public discussion of what we even mean by a "good" or "bad" sentence. And only by deciding that question can we begin to think seriously about what other reforms are necessary in the criminal courts.

For example, one way of defining a good sentence is to say it is that disposition that minimizes the chance of a given offender's repeating his crime. Under that definition, we would not only expect but want disparities in sentences—one armed robber getting five years in prison and another getting probation—provided only that we had good reason to believe that each sentence was appropriate to each criminal's prospects for rehabilitation. On the other hand, if we believe that a good sentence is one which deters others from committing a crime, then we might wish to impose the same penalty on persons with very different prospects for rehabilitation, and to make that penalty sufficiently severe to discourage potential criminals, especially those who believe they might be regarded as good bets for rehabilitative—which is to say, lenient—treatment.

A crucial question in deciding what is a good sentence, then, is what effect any given sentence will have on actual or potential offenders. It is not the only crucial question: We also want, or ought to want, sentences to give appropriate expression to our moral concern over the nature of the offense and to conform to our standards of humane conduct. But these latter standards, though inevitably matters of controversy, are ones which, even if met, would still leave a substantial zone of discretion to the judge.

Persons will differ over how they would resolve these issues, but whatever definition of a good sentence one adopts, it is unlikely that it will be descriptive of what is in fact happening in our criminal courts today. It is not too much to say that many sentences being administered are, in the strict sense, irrational—that is, there is no coherent goal toward which they are directed.

For example, Martin A. Levin of Brandeis University found in a study of the Pittsburgh Common Pleas Court in 1966 that well over one-half the white males convicted of burglary, grand larceny, indecent assault, or possession of narcotics, and who had a prior record, were placed on probation; nearly one-half of the two-time losers convicted of aggravated assault were also placed on probation, as were more than one-fourth of those convicted of robbery.[6] In Wisconsin, Dean V. Babst and John W. Mannering found that 63 per cent of the adult males convicted of a felony during 1954–1959 who had previously been convicted of another felony were placed on probation, and 41 per cent of those with two or more felony convictions were given probation for the subsequent offense.[7] In Los Angeles, only 6 per cent of those charged with burglary, who had a serious prior record, were sent to prison; only 12 per cent of those charged with burglary who had already *been* in prison were sent back.[8]

The judges did not seem to operate on either the deterrence or the rehabilitation theory of sentencing—the low proportion of jail sentences for persons convicted of serious crimes who had prior convictions suggests that the judges did not believe jail had a deterrent effect, and the fact that the men were convicted after an earlier offense implies that for them, at least, there had been no rehabilitation.

The treatment of persons in organized crime is even harder to reconcile with some theory of justice. Between 1963 and 1969, the number of persons arrested in New York State on felony narcotics charges (these typically were dealers, not merely users) increased by more than 700 per cent, and the number convicted more than tripled. But the number going to state prison remained unchanged, and thus the proportion going to prison fell from 68 per cent of those convicted to less than 23 per cent.[9] Being essentially businessmen (and businesswomen), members of organized crime are even less likely than youthful brawlers or addict thieves to be likely prospects for rehabilitation: They are acting, not out of passion or compulsion, but out of calculation. And in many jurisdictions those who can calculate best have seen the costs of their criminal ventures decline and the profits boom.

In Boston the average penalty in heroin cases fell during the 1960s—at the very time heroin abuse was rising. Between 1963 and 1970, the proportion of heroin cases before the Suffolk County (Boston) district and superior courts resulting in prison sentences fell from almost one-half to about one-tenth; meanwhile, the estimated number of heroin users rose from fewer than one thousand to almost six thousand. This pattern of sentencing can be explained by neither a deterrence nor a rehabilitation philosophy: Obviously the decrease in penalties did not deter heroin dealers, and the absence during most of this time of any treatment alternative to prison for heroin users meant that rehabilitation, if it were to occur at all, would have to occur spontaneously (which, of course, it did not).[10]

The reasons for the sentencing patterns in many courts have little or nothing to do with achieving some general social objective, but a great deal to do with the immediate problems and idiosyncratic beliefs of the judges. A few sentences can be explained by corruption, many more by the growing belief among some judges that since prisons apparently do not rehabilitate, it is wrong to send criminals to them, and most of all by the overwhelming need in busy jurisdictions to clear crowded court dockets.

When thousands of felony cases must be settled each year in a court, there are overpowering pressures to settle them on the basis of plea bargaining in order to avoid the time and expense of a trial. The defendant is offered a reduced charge or a lighter sentence in exchange for a plea of guilty. Though congested dockets are not the only reason for this practice, an increase in congestion increases the incentives for such bargaining and thus may increase the proportion of lighter sentences. For those who believe in the deterrence theory of sentencing, it is a grim irony: The more crime increases, the more the pressure on court calendars, and the greater the chances that the response to the crime increase will be a sentence decrease.

But the use of probation and suspended sentences also reflects the belief of growing numbers of judges that the purpose of prisons is to rehabilitate, that the prisons have failed in this assignment, and that a criminal kept out of prison has at least as good or a better chance to stop stealing as one sent away. And there is some evidence to support this point of view. In a recent review of the studies of persons on probation, Levin concluded that they "all indicate that offenders who have received probation generally have significantly lower rates of recidivism (i.e., are less likely to be arrested for, or convicted of, a subsequent offense) than those who have been incarcerated." Furthermore, of those who are incarcerated, those receiving shorter sentences are somewhat less likely to become repeaters than those who have received longer sentences.[11]

Perhaps the most comprehensive of these studies is one completed in California in 1970 by Ronald H. Beattie and Charles K. Bridges. It found that almost two-thirds of those offenders placed on probation had, one year later, no known subsequent arrest, while less than one-half of those sent to prison had been equally successful. These differences in "success" persisted even when one took into account the sex, age, race, offense, and prior record of the offender.[12]

The policy implications of such studies are not clear, however. Naturally probationers succeeded more than did prisoners—they were selected for probation precisely because the judges thought they would succeed. Putting more offenders now sent to prison on probation would not necessarily lead to better results; it would simply put the poorer risks on the street, with a consequent increase in the overall failure rate of probationers. If probation success rates now appear good, it is only because judges are good at guessing who will be successful.[13]

In fact, in New York, where the proportion of juveniles on probation has been going up, a *New York Times* survey in 1972 suggests that the failure rate has also been going up.[14] And it might be going up even more if we knew for certain how many persons on probation were actually breaking the law, but we don't—we know only how many are caught breaking the law, and that is probably only a small fraction of the total.

There have been very few efforts to put probation to the crucial test by assigning offenders randomly to probation and prison and then comparing the results. Perhaps the best known of these is the California Treatment Project (sometimes called the Warren study). President Johnson's crime commission singled out this experiment for special mention as evidence that rehabilitation was possible, especially if done in a community rather than institutional setting.[15] Young offenders, classified by their level of "interpersonal maturity," were assigned directly to probation officers in small groups and exposed to intensive and individually tailored therapy programs. Warren reported, and the crime commission repeated, the claim that these youth were much less likely to commit additional crimes than a similar group sent through the regular detention facilities and then placed in conventional probation. Upon later and closer study, however, it became clear that the experimental group not only did not commit fewer offenses, they committed *more.* Probation officers assigned to the experimental group were not revoking probation when young people in that group committed new offenses, while probation officers assigned to the regular youth (the "control group") were revoking probation in the normal way whenever a new offense was committed. In short, the "treatment" program did not alter the behavior of the delinquents, it only altered the behavior of the probation officers.[16]

In any event, most judges do not have a California Treatment Program to which they can sentence offenders. In most courts the practical choices are between routine probation (involving few services) and jail or prisons with varying degrees of security and amenity. And here the evidence seems quite clear: In general, different kinds of institutions do not make an appreciable difference in the prospects of rehabilitation.

Between 1966 and 1972, Robert Martinson reviewed, initially at the request of the New York State Governor's Committee on Criminal Offenders, 231 experimental studies on the treatment of criminals, including in this list *all* those from here and abroad that were available in print between 1945 and 1967 and that met various tests of methodological adequacy. Martinson's review came to a clear conclusion: "With few and isolated exceptions, the rehabilitative efforts that have been reported so far have no appreciable effect on recidivism." [17] Studies done since 1967 do not provide grounds for altering that conclusion significantly.

It does not seem to matter what form of treatment in the correctional system is attempted—whether vocational training or academic education; whether counseling inmates individually, in groups, or not at all; whether therapy is administered by social workers or psychiatrists; whether the institutional context of the treatment is custodial or benign; whether the sentences are short or long; whether the person is placed on probation or released on parole; or whether the treatment takes place in the community or in institutions. Indeed, some forms of treatment—notably a few experiments with psychotherapy—actually produced an *increase* in the rate of recidivism.

The Martinson review is unique in its comprehensiveness but not in its findings. R. G. Hood came to much the same conclusion in a review published in 1967; [18] Walter C. Bailey, after examining 100 studies of the efficacy of treatment and especially the 50 or so that claimed positive results, concluded in 1966 that the "evidence supporting the efficacy of correctional treatment is slight, inconsistent, and of questionable reliability"; [19] Leslie T. Wilkins observed in 1969 that "the major achievement of research in the field of social psychology and treatment has been negative and has resulted in the undermining of nearly all the current mythology regarding the effectiveness of treatment in any form." [20]

In retrospect, little of this should have been surprising. It requires not merely optimistic but heroic assumptions about the nature of man to lead one to suppose that a person, finally sentenced after (in most cases) many brushes with the law, and having devoted a good part of his youth and young adulthood to misbehavior of every sort, should, by either the solemnity of prison or the skillfulness of a counselor, come to see the error of his ways and to experience a transformation of his character. Today we smile in amusement at the naïveté of those early prison reformers who imagined that religious instruction while in solitary confinement would lead to moral regeneration. How they would now smile at us at our presumption that conversations with a psychiatrist or a return to the community could achieve the same end. We have learned how difficult it is by governmental means to improve the educational attainments of children or to restore stability and affection to the family, and in these cases we are often working with willing subjects in moments of admitted need. Criminal rehabilitation requires producing equivalent changes in unwilling subjects under conditions of duress or indifference.

The plight of the criminal court judge is obvious. Should he sentence a person to an institution that does not have a demonstrable effect on his criminality, or place him on probation, not knowing whether that will have any effect either? Even more important, should he take into account the characteristics of the offender in deciding on his prospects for rehabilitation, giving those with the best prospects (as predicted from age, sex, race, and prior record) the shortest sentences and those with the worst prospects the longest ones?

A moment's thought on such issues leads one squarely into the philosophical problem with the rehabilitation theory of sentencing. If rehabilitation is the object, and if there is little or no evidence that available correctional systems will produce much rehabilitation, why should any offenders be sent to any institutions? But to turn them free on the grounds that society does not know how to make them better is to fail to protect society from those crimes they may commit again and to violate society's moral concern for criminality, and thus to undermine society's concept of what constitutes proper conduct.

Furthermore, if rehabilitation is the goal, and persons differ in their capacity to be rehabilitated, then two persons who have committed precisely the same crime under precisely the same circumstances might receive very different sentences, thereby violating the offenders' and our sense of justice. The indeterminate sentence, widely used in many states, is expressive of the rehabilitation ideal: A convict will be released from an institution, not at the end of a fixed period, but when someone (a parole board, a sentencing board) decides he is "ready" to be released. Rigorously applied on the basis of existing evidence about what factors are associated with recidivism, this theory would mean that if two persons together rob a liquor store, the one who is a young black male from a broken family, with little education and a record of drug abuse, will be kept in prison indefinitely, while an older white male from an intact family, with a high school diploma and no drug experience, will be released almost immediately. Not only the young black male, but most fair-minded observers, would regard that outcome as profoundly unjust.

In practice, the system does not work as its theory implies. But neither does it work well. The decision when to release a prison inmate is, in many states, given over to a parole board from which few if any appeals are possible. In New York State, for example, the twelve members of the board of parole have jurisdiction over all prisoners serving more than ninety days (a total well in excess of twenty thousand) and can, among other things, decide when to release a prisoner who is serving an indeterminate sentence. Supposedly the board examines all aspects of the prisoner's life and behavior to decide if he is "ready" for release. If it were capable of and had the time for such profound judgments, it might well behave in the way described in the liquor store example above. But of course no board can make profound judgments about the thousands of cases it hears every year, with the result that it adopts instead a rule of thumb: If a prisoner is thought to be "rehabilitated," he will be released when he has served one-third of his sentence or three years, whichever is less. The board decides who is rehabilitated and who is not by reviewing a file of reports and questioning the inmate for ten or fifteen minutes at an interview. If parole is denied, the inmate is not told the reason; if he objects, there is no appeal.

The Citizen's Inquiry on Parole and Criminal Justice in New York City prepared in 1974 a study of the results of this parole system. For a four-year period, the percentage of prisoners returned to prison within one year was calculated for those who were granted parole and those who, by being denied parole, were required to serve their full sentence. Overall, there was no statistically significant difference between the return to prison rates of those paroled and those not—about 10 or 11 per cent of each group went back to prison within the year.[21] Clearly, the parole board was unable to guess who had been rehabilitated and who had not.

Now suppose we abandon entirely the rehabilitation theory of sentencing and corrections—not the effort to rehabilitate, just the theory that the governing purpose of the enterprise is to rehabilitate. We could continue experiments with new correctional and therapeutic procedures, expanding them when the evidence warrants. If existing correctional programs do not differ in their rehabilitative potential, we could support those that are least costly and most humane (while still providing reasonable security) and phase out those that are most costly and inhumane. But we would not do any of these things on the mistaken notion that we were thereby reducing recidivism.

Instead, we would view the correctional system as having a very different function—namely, to isolate and to punish. It is a measure of our confusion that such a statement will strike many enlightened readers today as cruel, even barbaric. It is not. It is merely a recognition that society at a minimum must be able to protect itself from dangerous offenders and to impose some costs (other than the stigma and inconvenience of an arrest and court appearance) on criminal acts; it is also a frank admission that society really does not know how to do much else.

The purpose of isolating—or, more accurately, closely supervising—offenders is obvious: Whatever they may do when they are released, they cannot harm society while confined or closely supervised. The gains from merely incapacitating convicted criminals may be very large. (In the last chapter I refer to some tentative estimates of their magnitude.) If much or most serious crime is committed by repeaters, separating repeaters from the rest of society, even for relatively brief periods of time, may produce major reductions in crime rates. Yet we have pursued virtually the opposite policy. During the 1960s, while crime rates were soaring, there was no significant increase in the amount of prison space and there was an actual decline in the number of prisoners, state and federal, from about 213,000 in 1960 to 196,000 in 1970.[22] In New York State the chances of the perpetrator of a given crime going to prison fell during this period by a factor of *six.*[23] To an astonishing degree, judges and prosecutors have used their discretion to minimize the incapacitative value of prisons. In Los Angeles County, for example, the proportion of convicted robbers with a major prior record who were sent to prison in 1970 was only 27 per cent.[24] It is no defense of this policy of deprisonization to say that criminals, if sent to prison, would, on their release, merely resume the commission of crimes. Many no doubt would, but the gains to society from crimes not committed while they were in prison would be real and substantial, and if the policy of prison sentences were consistently followed, even with relatively short (one or two years) sentences, the gains would be enduring.

These gains would exist even if the prospect of going to prison deterred no one from committing a crime. And clearly that prospect has not deterred those who have already found their way into prison. But suppose the probability of imprisonment were increased: Might there not be a reduction in crime owing to the greater deterrent value of prison as well as a gain resulting from its incapacitative effect?

Over the last few years, several efforts have been made to assess the deterrent effect of sentences. These efforts are not immune to criticism: They are based on police reports of crimes committed (which are in error to some degree), they are based on comparison of sentencing behavior among states (which are very large units within which much variation no doubt occurs), and they are not experimental studies (that is, they do not show what happens when one deliberately changes the pattern of sentencing while holding everything else constant). Nonetheless, since all the studies come more or less to the same conclusion, and since the statistical techniques used make it unlikely that the results could be due to chance, the general thrust of these studies is revealing.

George E. Antunes of Rice University and A. Lee Hunt of the University of Houston have reviewed several studies which estimate the effect on crime rates of the certainty and the severity of punishment. "Certainty" was measured by dividing the number of persons sent to prison in each state for a given crime in a given year by the number of those crimes reported to the police in that state in the preceding years. The larger the proportion of reported crimes resulting in imprisonment, the greater the certainty of punishment. "Severity" was the median length of a prison sentence (in months or years) imposed in a given state for a given crime. The longer the sentence, the more severe it is (capital punishment was ignored in these studies). All the studies suggested that the certainty of punishment has a significant deterrent effect on crime rates, while severity has such an effect only on murder.[25]

Isaac Ehrlich of the University of Chicago has carried out the most detailed statistical analysis of the effects of criminal sanctions. For 1940, 1950, and 1960, he calculated the effect on the known rates of seven major crimes of the probability of imprisonment and the length of imprisonment. He controlled for the effects of such factors as family income and the percentage of a state's population that was nonwhite. Unlike the studies summarized by Antunes and Hunt, he concluded that *both* an increased certainty of a sentence and an increased length of sentence reduced the rate of reported crimes in the states.[26]

It is not entirely clear whether the crime reduction associated with lengthy prison terms, found by Ehrlich, is the result of the deterrent effect of those terms on would-be criminals who are contemplating imprisonment, or the incapacitating effect of those terms on would-be recidivists who are languishing in prison. Ehrlich's data are also consistent with the view that punishment deters to some degree crimes of passion as well as crimes of profit.

Though Ehrlich's findings are not entirely consistent with those of others, at least with respect to the effects of severity of sentence, reconciling these various studies is less important, and perhaps less difficult, than persuading informed persons to take them seriously. What is remarkable is that so few knowledgeable persons, especially among the ranks of many professional students of crime, are even willing to entertain the possibility that penalties make a difference. We have become so preoccupied with dealing with the causes of the crime (whether the causes are thought to be social conditions or police inadequacies) that we have almost succeeded in persuading ourselves that criminals are radically different from ordinary people—that they are utterly indifferent to the costs and rewards of their activities, and are responding only to deep passions, fleeting impulses, or uncontrollable social forces.

There is scarcely any evidence to support the proposition that would-be criminals are indifferent to the risks associated with a proposed course of action. Criminals may be willing to run greater risks (or they may have a weaker sense of morality) than the average citizen, but if the expected cost of crime goes up without a corresponding increase in the expected benefits, then the would-be criminal—unless he or she is among that small fraction of criminals who are utterly irrational—engages in less crime, just as the average citizen will be less likely to take a job as a day laborer if the earnings from that occupation, relative to those from other occupations, go down.

Most of us are prepared to accept the notion that effective application of penalties, even rather modest ones, will deter certain forms of behavior. Everyone who has traveled to Los Angeles from the East Coast observes with awe the extent to which routine traffic laws, including those against jaywalking, are obeyed. The explanation is obvious: For decades, the police have enforced those laws with sufficient vigor to make the average Angeleno feel that the risks of breaking the law are sufficiently great, and the costs of observing the law sufficiently small, to make it worthwhile to obey. The enforcement of laws against drunken driving in Scandinavia has reduced substantially the number of persons who drive after drinking. The passing of bad checks in various states was found in one study to be related to the vigor of enforcement efforts.[27]

But while most of us are prepared to concede all this, many of us are reluctant to apply the same analysis to more serious forms of crime—apparently on the unstated assumption that traffic laws, jaywalking ordinances, and bad-check statutes are primarily enforced against middle-class people who are more "rational" than the lower-class people who commit "real" crimes. Obviously not all criminals are sensitive to costs and benefits. Some husbands will murder their wives though they are almost certain to be caught, some boys will steal cars in order to prove that they are not afraid of the police, and some madmen will plant bombs that destroy themselves as well as their victims. But this is not very different from observing that some men go on buying big, powerful cars even though the price of gasoline and auto repairs has skyrocketed and their resale value has plummeted. To understand such people, we might want to know whether they have large families, a need to prove their masculinity, or a desire to impress their neighbors. But however interesting we found this speculation, we would not for a moment doubt that, for most people most of the time, the cost of cars is an important factor in predicting their automotive purchases.

The deterrent capacity of criminal penalties is supported by statistical data for large numbers of offenses over long periods of time. Such a theory does not, however, purport to "explain" crime. As argued in Chapter 3, the intellectual process of explanation is not the same as that of policy analysis, and can lead to quite different results. For example, a hundred persons may confront equal prospective benefits (say, having $1,000 stolen from a bank) and equal prospective costs (say, a one in five chance of imprisonment), but ninety-five will not seriously consider bank robbery, while five will pull a gun and march up to the cashier without a moment's hesitation. It is intellectually interesting to try to discover why the five steal and the ninety-five do not; no doubt it has much to do with their tolerance of risk or their values as shaped by family, friends, and media. From the point of view of public policy, however, such explanations are of little value, because government has no way of changing in any systematic fashion family backgrounds, deep-seated attitudes, friendship patterns, or media images. And even if government could do these things, the cost would be frightful—not only in money terms, because the programs would have to be directed at the ninety-five who are not likely to be criminal in order to be certain of reaching the five who are, but also in terms of those fundamental human values that would be jeopardized if government possessed the capacity to direct the inner life of the family or to mold the mental state of its citizens.

What the government can do is to change the risks of robbery and the rewards of alternative sources of income for those who, at the margin, are neither hopelessly addicted to thievery nor morally vaccinated against it, and to incapacitate, by prison or some other form of close supervision, those who rob despite the threats and alternatives society provides.

Several studies have suggested that property crime increases with increases in unemployment; this was the conclusion of Belton Fleisher after analyzing juvenile arrest rates and the finding of Phillips, Votey, and Maxwell using somewhat different data.[28] Isaac Ehrlich, in the most sophisticated statistical analysis of state crime rates made to date, showed that unemployment and various other measures of economic need tended to increase crime while the certainty of punishment tended to lessen it.[29] This suggests that simultaneously decreasing teenage unemployment and increasing the risks of youthful crime may be the most rational response society can make to property crime.

Even if increasing the certainty of a prison sentence is valuable both for its deterrent as well as for its incapacitative effect, we must still consider the problem of how long a sentence should be imposed. This is a complex question. Humanity and a sense of proportion require us to make the penalty commensurate with the gravity of the offense—ten years in jail for stealing five dollars would be clearly outlandish. Even so, one must concede that in any rational system of criminal justice it will always be necessary to have some very severe penalties, even if they have no deterrent effect on crime. In the first place, the moral horror of certain offenses is such that society would not—and probably should not—tolerate the imposition of small penalties even if larger ones do not increase the deterrent effect. As the English legal philosopher James Fitzjames Stephens observed in the nineteenth century, if murder could be prevented by the fine of one shilling, we could not without doing violence to the moral bonds of society settle for a one-shilling fine for murderers.[30]

In the second place, there must always be a penalty that can be imposed on persons who, while serving the maximum existing penalty, commit another crime—for example, a convict serving a long prison sentence who kills a prison guard. Some ultimate penalty must always exist to help protect innocent persons from criminals who "have nothing to lose." Third, the threat of severe penalties is an important resource for investigators seeking to obtain criminal informers. If those who inform on a ring of heroin dealers risk death, while those who deal in heroin risk only one year in prison, few dealers will become police informers—avoiding a one-year sentence is not worth the chance of assassination. But if the sentence they avoid is five or ten years, many more pushers will be willing to run at least a reasonable risk of being murdered.

Finally, it is possible that in particular cases very severe penalties are a deterrent, though statistically, severity seems related only to the deterrence of murder.

But even if all of these arguments are correct, there are at least two considerations that should lead us to conclude that severe penalties cannot be the norm. First, except in unusual cases, severity is probably subject to rapidly diminishing returns. The difference between a one-year and a five-year sentence is likely to appear very great to a convict, but the difference between a twenty-year and a twenty-five-year sentence (or even a thirty-year sentence) is likely to appear rather small. Second, the more severe the penalty, the more unlikely that it will be imposed. To ensure a conviction, avoid an expensive trial, reduce the chances of reversal on appeal, and give expression to their own views of benevolence, prosecutors and judges will try to get a guilty plea, and all they can offer in return is a lesser sentence. The more severe the sentence, the greater the bargaining power of the accused, and the greater the likelihood he will be charged with a lesser offense. Extremely long mandatory minimum sentences do not always strengthen the hand of society; they often strengthen the hand of the criminal instead.

If this analysis is correct, what does it imply for the criminal court system? In an ideal world, it would imply something like the following:

First, the court system would be organized around the primary task of sentencing, not around the largely mythic task of determining guilt. Hearings and trials under strict standards of due process would still be held, of course, where the issue of guilt is in doubt, but (again, in the ideal world) this would occupy only a fraction of the courts' resources and perhaps be handled by judges who specialized in that work.

Second, the sentencing process would be placed under central management, with uniform standards enforced by a presiding officer and applied under his direction.

Third, every conviction for a nontrivial offense would entail a penalty that involved a deprivation of liberty, even if brief. For many offenses the minimum sentence might be as low as one week, and even that might be served on weekends. For most offenses the average sentence would be relatively short—perhaps no more than six months or a year—but it would be invariably applied. Only the most serious offenses would result in long penalties.

Fourth, "deprivation of liberty" need not, and usually would not, entail confinement in a conventional prison. After the deprivation of liberty is decided upon, a decision would be made as to whether it would involve confinement at night and on weekends, while allowing a person to work during the day; enrollment in a closely supervised community-based treatment program; referral to a narcotics treatment program; or confinement in a well-guarded prison. Judgment as to the form the deprivation would take would be based on the need to protect society and on the prospects of the offender for rehabilitation. But the prospects for rehabilitation should not be allowed to govern the length of sentence, nor whether there should be some deprivation of liberty: To permit the former would be unjust to the offender, to permit the latter would be unjust to society. Conventional probation—releasing an offender on the understanding that occasionally he would visit his probation officer—would be virtually abolished.

Fifth, conviction for a subsequent offense would invariably result in an increased deprivation of liberty. If the second offense were minor, the increase would be small; if grave, the increase would be substantial. Whatever the case, something would be done. Penalties would be primarily designed to fit the crime, with some (but not much) range for judicial discretion in order that mitigating and exacerbating circumstances might be taken into account.

Such proposals will be opposed by judges unwilling to surrender their authority to do as they please; by legislators who feel that it is necessary to pass bills requiring massive sentences that are rarely imposed; by taxpayers' groups that do not wish to foot the bill for the substantial additional expenditures required for new correctional facilities and more court and correctional personnel; and by those who feel that punishment does not work, or that, whether it works or not, it is wrong to apply it to criminals until society itself has been punished for "producing" criminals.

If the opposition of these groups could be overcome, there would be problems in administering the new system. If every offender knew that some penalty would befall him, he might have less incentive to plead guilty, and thus would demand a trial, thereby changing the mythic function of the courts into the real one, and so paralyzing them. (In fact, I would guess that many offenders would prefer the certainty of a relatively short sentence to the cost of a trial and the possibility of a longer or more confining sentence which might result from revelations during the trial of the full range of evidence against him and of the nature of his character.)

What in fact would happen could only be learned by experience, but the inertia of the present system coupled with the myopic view that judges and correctional officers are capable of transforming human character are, unfortunately, powerful impediments to our ever acquiring that experience. Formidable as these barriers are, there is an even greater one—namely, the widespread view that hiring more judges but giving them less discretion, and building more correctional facilities, albeit decent and humane ones, are at best a confession of social failure and at worst a blindly repressive act.

I regard these actions as neither. Our society has been, with individual exceptions, remarkably forebearing. We have preserved and extended the most comprehensive array of civil liberties to be found in almost any nation, despite a rising crime rate and (during the 1960s) periods of massive social disorder. No nation that can so value human liberty and be so willing to check governmental power, even at some substantial cost in domestic tranquillity, can be accused of placing convenience, privilege, and security over all other considerations. Arrests are far easier and trials less encumbered with evidentiary rules in most other nations, including those, such as Great Britain, which we acknowledge to be bastions of freedom. If we choose to have a comprehensive bill of rights, as I think we should, we should be willing to pay the price of that choice. That price includes a willingness to accept both a higher level of crime and disorder and a larger investment in the resources and facilities needed to cope with those who violate the law and, despite our procedural guarantees, are caught by its agents.

Nor can a greater investment in criminal justice facilities be thought repressive if one compares what is with what might be. Crowded, antiquated prisons that require men and women to live in fear of one another and to suffer not only deprivation of liberty but a brutalizing regimen are hardly preferable to modern facilities that insure a modicum of privacy and in which security can be insured. What *is* illiberal and ungenerous is either to preserve the status quo or to insist that all prisons be closed, whatever the price in increased victimization.

Chapter 9

The Death Penalty

IN 1972 the United States Supreme Court, by a vote of five to four, held that the death penalty as then imposed was a "cruel and unusual punishment" and thus a violation of the Eighth Amendment to the Constitution.[1] Not everyone could agree on what the Court meant to say—each of the nine justices wrote a separate opinion—but many concluded that the Court's chief objection was to the arbitrary and capricious imposition of the death penalty. Thus many inferred that the Court might accept a law that made the death penalty "automatic" for specified crimes. President Nixon in 1973 submitted to Congress a proposal that would authorize imposition of the death penalty under fairly clear standards for certain federal offenses (for example, war-related treason, sabotage and espionage, and particular crimes from which victims die).

Meanwhile, several states have reinstated the death penalty in ways designed to meet what they take to be the Supreme Court's objections, usually by limiting executions to certain major but relatively uncommon offenses (for example, killing a police officer) or by reducing judicial discretion in imposing death sentences so as to avoid charges of arbitrariness. As of October

1974, twenty-nine states had already restored the death penalty, and several more have moved to do so. Former Governor Nelson Rockefeller of New York promised to seek the restoration of the death penalty, in ways that would eliminate its discretionary nature, for the murder of police officers and prison guards. At least 147 persons have been sentenced to death, mostly in the South.

In short, the Supreme Court decision has not settled much. Indeed, in a curious way, it has had the opposite effect of what many who favor abolishing the death penalty had hoped. By appearing to base its judgment on the slow and uncertain way in which the death penalty has been imposed, the Court has focused attention on the possibility of making death mandatory for various offenses. For decades the death penalty was slowly withering away as judges and juries exercised ever more discretion in reaching their verdicts in capital cases. This withering away pleased abolitionists, though of course they wished it would proceed even faster. And as executions became less common, they seemed to become more arbitrary. The result, it was supposed, would be a Court-imposed end to all executions under any circumstances. Instead we have a rush of new laws that may well rescue, by making more predictable, the use of capital punishment. As a result, capital punishment must now be debated anew, on the merits, without recourse to the easy assumption that capricious administration would accomplish what appeals to public opinion could not.

The death penalty can be defended or criticized on grounds of either justice or utility. By "justice" I mean considerations of fitness and fairness: death either is or is not a fitting, appropriate, or necessary punishment for those who commit certain kinds of crimes, and such punishment either can or cannot be fairly administered. The biblical injunction, "an eye for an eye," is an argument for death (or at least maiming) on grounds of justice; so also is the argument that the supreme penalty is the only appropriate response to the supreme crime because we

184

cheapen the value of human life if an innocent victim dies while his convicted murderer lives.

Appeals to justice can also be used to argue for abolition of the death penalty. Human life is sacred and may never be taken deliberately, even by the state. Further, society ought not to encourage sentiments of vengeance or cater to morbid interest in ritual executions. Moreover, no penalty is acceptable if it is administered in ways that are grossly unfair; in this country, at least, certain disadvantaged groups have experienced a disproportionate number of executions.

The argument on grounds of justice is certainly the most profound and to me the most interesting. As I shall suggest in the course of this discussion, it may be the only proper basis for a decision. And at one time, discussion of capital punishment was often based entirely on considerations of justice and morality. The most striking aspect of contemporary discussions of this issue, however, is that, except for the fairness question, they almost never proceed along moral lines. And for opponents of capital punishment, the assertion that it is imposed unfairly seems their weakest argument, for it might be answered by making executions mandatory for those convicted of the relevant crimes. This was the case in England, for example, where, until hanging was abolished, the judge was required to sentence to death any person convicted of murder (all murder was the same, there being no distinction, as here, between first and second degree homicide).

Perhaps because we find it hard to argue about first principles, perhaps because our leaders and spokesmen are untrained in the discipline of philosophic discourse, perhaps because we are an increasingly secular and positivist society that has little confidence in its ethical premises, the capital punishment debate has been framed largely in utilitarian terms. Most of the literature, in short, does not explore the moral worth or evil of execution so much as the consequences of executions for other parties, or for society at large. The utility of capital punishment can depend on several considerations: Executions are cheaper than confinement in prison for long terms; an executed man cannot commit additional crimes; and executions deter others from committing certain crimes. The first two utilitarian reasons are rarely taken seriously; we usually assume that cost (within reason) should make no difference when a human life is at stake, and that life imprisonment can prevent the convicted person from committing additional crimes as surely as execution. In fact, the alternative to execution is not often, or even usually, life imprisonment, but in many states a life sentence with eligibility for parole in three to five years. For example, the median time served in prison for homicide in Massachusetts is less than two and a half years.

Though it need not be so, the utilitarian argument is in practice an argument over deterrence, and deterrence is not a simple issue. This may be illustrated, to begin with, by considering the problem of placing the burden of proof. Proponents of the death penalty claim that those who favor its abolition must show that it does not deter criminals, while opponents argue that those who defend capital punishment must prove that it *does* have a deterrent effect. In one of the better debates, sociologist Ernest van den Haag and Hugo Adam Bedau, professor of philosophy at Tufts University, faced this issue squarely. Writing in *Ethics* in 1968, van den Haag argued that the burden of proof should fall on the abolitionists.[2] He admitted that society faces the risk of executing persons even though the executions might not deter any potential murderer—or at least would not deter him more than would the possibility of life imprisonment. But he pointed out that society also faces the risk of not executing a convicted murderer when such executions would in fact have deterred other murderers. The choice, he argued, is not between a safe and a risky course of action, but between two risky ones. For van den Haag, the risk of allowing future innocent victims to be killed by murderers who would have been deterred by capital punishment was far graver than the risk of executing a convicted murderer whose death deters no one. Since the cost to society is greater if we wrongly reject the deterrence theory than if we wrongly accept it, he argued that those who favor rejecting it ought to be required to prove that it does not work.

Bedau saw the matter quite differently. Writing in 1970, he argued (and up to a point van den Haag would agree) that the issue is not whether the death penalty deters would-be murderers, but whether it deters them more than the prospect of life imprisonment.[3] It is a matter of dispute whether any penalty will have a deterrent effect on murderers, but surely the prospect of a long prison term will have as much as most others. For the death penalty to be warranted, it would have to supply an additional increment of deterrence sufficient to offset the costs of imposing it, those costs being the risk of executing an innocent man, the opportunities for discrimination in imposing the penalty, and the foregone possibility of rehabilitating the murderer. Fairness would always be a problem, he notes, because, though imposition of the death penalty could be made mandatory, juries in such cases might be unwilling to convict at all for fear of convicting wrongly.

Here it is interesting to note that in Great Britain, where judges had less discretion in imposing the death penalty than they do in the United States, the number of murderers found insane—and so spared the gallows—dropped sharply after the death penalty was abolished in 1965. It is hard to believe that there were fewer insane persons in Britain after abolition of the death penalty; what apparently happened was that the authorities no longer felt it as necessary to protect the accused from penalties when the penalty was no longer death. No one should assume that any judicial outcome can be made truly "mandatory"—discretion removed from one place in the criminal justice system tends to reappear elsewhere in it.

However academic it may seem, such a debate is useful in that it reveals to us that we can make proper judgments about deterrence only if we have first come to some firm conclusions about the costs and benefits of executions. But the scholarship to date shows that such conclusions are elusive.

The chief cost of the death penalty is thought to be the possibility of executing an innocent man erroneously. But even as ardent an abolitionist as Bedau does not claim that we have paid that cost very often. In 1962 he compiled a list of seventy-four cases since 1893 in which a wrongful conviction for murder is alleged to have occurred in this country. No one should assume that this is a complete list, but it includes all that had been turned up until then. In only eight of the seventy-four cases was the death sentence carried out (there have been more than seven thousand executions in this century); in the majority of cases no death sentence was even imposed.[4] Writing in 1971, Bedau stated that no further instances of erroneous execution had occurred since his earlier review and concluded that it is "false sentimentality to argue that the death penalty should be abolished because of the abstract possibility that an innocent person might be executed, when the record fails to disclose that such cases occur." [5]

The other major cost is the inequity of having certain kinds of persons suffer the death penalty disproportionately. In the North, it is not entirely clear whether certain groups have been unfairly treated. The mere fact that most persons executed are black or poor is not conclusive, since murder occurs disproportionately, for various reasons, among the poor and the black. The best study is probably that of Marvin Wolfgang, professor of sociology at the University of Pennsylvania, and associates in 1962.[6] The four hundred thirty-nine persons sentenced to death for murder in Philadelphia between 1914 and 1958 were divided into two categories: those for whom the sentence was commuted and those who were actually executed. Blacks were somewhat more likely than whites to be executed, but the difference, while statistically significant, was not large (88 per cent of blacks, 80 per cent of whites were executed). Among those charged with felony murder (that is, with having caused a death that occurs in the course of committing another kind of crime, such as robbery, rape, or burglary), whites were three times as likely as blacks to have their sentences commuted. Occupation and social class did not seem to have much effect on one's chances of having his sentence commuted, but having a private lawyer (rather than a court-appointed one) did: Blacks having private counsel were much more likely to get a commutation than blacks having court counsel.

In the South, though, there seems to be fairly strong evidence that blacks, especially blacks who have murdered or raped a white person, were much more likely than whites, other things being equal, to be sentenced to death. The most comprehensive study of southern practices is that of Wolfgang and Professor Anthony Amsterdam of the University of Pennsylvania Law School.[7] They examined more than three thousand rape convictions in eleven southern states between 1945 and 1965. They found that a black convicted of rape was not likely to be executed (only 13 per cent were), but that blacks were almost seven times as likely to be executed as whites convicted of the same crime. And if the black had raped a white woman, he was eighteen times as likely to be executed as all other racial combinations of criminals and victims. These findings could not be explained away by any other circumstances of the crime. One assumes that in parts of the South, heavier penalties for blacks may be common for many offenses, and not just those punishable by death.

If the problem of fairness does exist, however, the importance of it is not particularly clear. For if capital punishment is to be abolished because it is discriminatory, should not all forms of punishment be abolished because they are discriminatory? The answer the abolitionists would give—though they rarely address the problem—is that we single out the death penalty for special judgment because alternatives (like prison) exist for it, because discrimination in prison terms can in principle be corrected by subsequent review and commutation, and because, while we may be powerless to end discrimination generally, we can at least prevent the worst consequences of it.

If these are the risks, however unclear, what about the benefits of capital punishment?

Here the problem becomes one of measuring its deterrent effects. Three things can be said about recent attempts to do so: (1) there is virtually no serious study that indicates that the death penalty is a deterrent above and beyond imprisonment; (2) none of these studies is sufficiently rigorous to prove beyond dispute the absence of deterrence; and (3) it is most unlikely we shall ever have a study that settles the matter one way or another, for the obstacles in the way of a conclusive study are probably insuperable.

Thorsten Sellin, emeritus professor of sociology at the University of Pennsylvania, has been responsible for the best-known of these studies.[8] He has compared homicide rates in four ways. First, he compared homicide rates between adjacent states with and without the death penalty. The crude rates for homicide in these groups of states appear to be about the same, and to change in the same ways, regardless of whether a state does or does not have the death penalty on the books. Second, he compared homicide rates within states before and after they abolished or restored the death penalty. The rates did not change significantly after the legal status of the penalties changed. Third, he examined homicide rates in those cities where executions occurred and were presumed to have been publicized. There was no difference in the homicide rate before and after the executions. (Similar studies, with similar results, were done by Robert Dann, Leonard D. Savitz, and William Graves.[9] Graves even uncovered evidence in California that led him to speculate that there was an increase in the number of homicides on the days immediately preceding an execution.) Finally, Sellin sought to discover whether law-enforcement officers were safer from murderous attacks in states with the death penalty than in those without it. He found that the rate at which police officers were shot and killed in states that had abolished capital punishment was the same as the rate in states that had retained the death penalty. Donald R. Campion reached the same conclusion after studying the deaths of state police officers.[10]

It is sometimes argued in rejoinder to these findings that

while executions may not deter murderers generally, they will help protect prison guards and other inmates from fatal assaults by convicts who "have nothing else to lose." Sellin compiled a list of fifty-nine persons who committed murders in state and federal prisons in 1965. He concluded that it is "visionary" to believe that the death penalty could reduce the "hazards of life in prison." Eleven of the prison murders were found in states without capital punishment and forty-three were in states with it. (The other five were in federal prisons.)

All these studies have serious methodological weaknesses. One problem is the degree of comparability of states with and without the death penalty. Sellin tried to "match" states by taking contiguous ones (for example, Michigan, Indiana, and Ohio), but of course such states are not really matched at all—they differ not only in the penalty for murder but in many other respects as well, and these other differences may offset any differences resulting from the form of punishment.

Another problem lies in the definition of a capital crime. What should be studied is the rate of crimes for which capital punishment is legally possible. I am not aware of any data on "murder rates" that distinguish between those homicides (like first-degree murder) for which death may be a penalty and those (like second-degree murder or non-negligent manslaughter) for which it may not. Sellin's studies compare homicide rates, but no one knows what fraction of those homicides are first-degree murders for which execution is possible, even in the states that retain capital punishment. Furthermore, death has been imposed to punish crimes other than homicides—for example, kidnapping, skyjacking, armed robbery, and assault by a life-term prisoner. These are scarcely ever studied, yet they are among the most feared crimes.

Finally, and perhaps most important, it is not clear from many of these studies what is meant by "the death penalty." If what is meant is simply the legal possibility of execution, then "the death penalty" may be more fiction than fact. In many states that have the death penalty on the books, no executions have been carried out for many years. The majority members of a legislative commission in Massachusetts, for example, reported in 1968 that the death penalty is no deterrent to crime, but the minority members pointed out that no one had been executed in the state since 1947, and therefore no one could say whether the legal possibility of execution was or was not a deterrent. Indeed, in 1960 there were only fifty-six executions in the entire country, more than half of these occurring in the South; in 1965 there were only seven, and there have been no executions since 1967, when there were two.[11] In short, the comparative studies have not distinguished carefully between states that abolished the death penalty de jure and those that abolished it de facto. And even in states that practice the death penalty, the chances of a murderer's being executed have been so small that a rational murderer might well decide to take the risk. There were eight thousand murders in 1960, but only fifty-six executions; thus, a murderer's chances of being executed were only about one in one hundred forty. After 1960 the number of executions dropped sharply, thus improving his chances. We have no way of knowing what the deterrent effect of capital punishment would have been in the last decade or two if the odds had been less in the murderer's favor.

At best, deterrence studies show that legally abolishing capital punishment in states that had only rarely imposed it does not lead to any increase in homicide, and that states that rarely execute murderers do not have any more murders than states that never do. The crucial question, at least for those debating the deterrence issue, is whether we can ever say any more than this.

I suspect that we will not be able to say much more. Such factors as region (the South has proportionately more murders than the North), race (blacks are more likely to murder, and to be murdered, than whites), and class (the poor are more likely to murder, and to be murdered, than the well-to-do) all contribute to the homicide rate. If these factors are taken into account in any statistical explanation of the murder rate, the additional importance of the death penalty, or its absence, to the analysis is likely to be slight.

Perhaps the only way to settle the matter would be by experiment—execute all the murderers in a random group of states, imprison all murderers in another random group, and observe the results over time. But such a thought serves only to illustrate the happy fact that the social sciences are rarely permitted the carefully controlled procedures of the physical sciences.

Some persons have tried to get at the question of deterrence by simply asking people whether they have been deterred. For example, one could ask criminals, or would-be criminals, how they perceived the consequences of acts they had committed or considered committing. These studies are at best inconclusive, at worst silly. The most common rely on the testimonies of prison wardens—former Warden Clinton Duffy of San Quentin, for example, who stated that the electric chair, or even prison itself, constitutes no deterrent because the "convicts have told me so again and again." [12] But obviously those in prison, or facing electrocution, have not been deterred; if they had, they would not be there to talk to the warden. Their statements say nothing about how many nonprisoners may have been deterred.

Another example of this approach was a survey conducted in 1971 by the Los Angeles Police Department. Persons arrested for violent crimes were interviewed to find out whether they were armed and, if not, why not. Of the ninety-nine individuals who either carried no weapon or carried one they did not use, half said that they had been deterred by fear of the death penalty. [13] (At that time California had ninety-four persons in prison under sentence of death, but only two had actually been executed since 1962.) It is as hard to give credence to the views of arrested criminals as to those of myopic wardens. Prisoners in the hands of the police are likely to tell the police what they think they want to hear, and the police are disproportionately inclined to favor the death penalty. Furthermore, even if the

193

data are correct, the best they show is that some people, under the mistaken belief that they might be executed, are reluctant to use guns in crimes.

The problem of deterrence has also been considered in light of the nature of murder and murderers. Franklin E. Zimring of the University of Chicago, in a detailed study of assault cases, has shown that sociologically, and probably also psychologically, assault and murder are indistinguishable events in a large proportion of the crimes—most murders are merely "successful" assaults. A typical assault is an encounter between persons known or related to each other in which rage, often stimulated by alcohol or sexual jealousy, leads to violence. Whether the violence leads to murder will often depend, Zimring has shown, on whether or not a weapon is present, and if present, whether it is a knife, a small-caliber gun, or large-caliber gun.[14]

Such crimes of passion are not, as some claim, undeterrable. Even enraged persons are aware that their acts have some consequences, and it seems safe to assume that many more barroom or bedroom fights would end with a weapon being used if there were no penalty for the offense. But whether the additional increment of deterrence provided by a death penalty would be significant is far from clear, especially since in this country we have not had and will not have in the future a criminal justice system that imposes death in more than a tiny fraction of homicides of this nature. It might be more useful, Zimring implies, to impose penalties in assault cases whose severity depends on the caliber of the weapon employed. Perhaps we should treat all kinds of assaults more seriously than we do now, instead of waiting until murder results. (An assault arising out of a domestic disturbance is likely to receive virtually no penalty under present circumstances.) By raising the price of cuttings and shootings, we might lower the incidence of these murders of passion. Indeed, basing penalties for assaults in part on the kind of weapon (if any) used might contribute more to gun control than passing unenforceable laws calling for civilian disarmament.

But what about murderers who exhibit a degree of calculation and premeditation? There are three kinds—the cold-blooded killer who intends and carefully contrives his victim's death, the maniacal killer who is irrational in every sense except his ability to arrange another person's demise, and the robber or arsonist who plots a property crime that results in the death of another person, with or without his intending it. The professional, the compulsive, and the felon murderer (or their counterparts in other major crimes, such as espionage, kidnapping, or hijacking) are the principal candidates for the death penalty. The criminal justice system already recognizes this: Setting aside the compulsive, who may be judged criminally insane and thus institutionalized, the courts impose especially severe penalties on professional, felon, or other calculating murderers such as assassins, terrorists, and kidnappers.

There is no evidence to indicate whether the state's power to punish such persons with death will or will not reduce the probability of these crimes. If the public and their elected officials are to make decisions on this matter, as they must, they will have to rely on their own best judgment. "Best judgment" means two things: how one thinks people will react to certain penalties and whether one thinks such penalties are fair and just. Social science can do little more than rule out certain sweeping generalizations, such as "We can prove that the death penalty deters."

If public opinion is to play a role in these matters, what can we expect of it? In 1964 the citizens of Oregon voted in a referendum to abolish the death penalty in that state, but in 1966 Colorado voters chose to retain its death penalty statute, as did the voters in Illinois in 1970. In a nonbinding referendum in 1968, Massachusetts voters expressed the view that they favored keeping capital punishment. These referenda were all broadly phrased, of course, and even if one accepts the results, they do not settle such issues as the circumstances under which death might be imposed.

Gallup Polls taken over several years indicate that support for the death penalty declined from 68 per cent in 1953 to 42 per cent in 1966. In that year a majority of those interviewed would have repealed the death penalty for murder. Perhaps because of the rise in crime rates during the late 1960s, support for capital punishment has gone up again slightly. In 1969, 51 per cent said they favored it. Young persons are more opposed to death penalties than older ones, and women more than men. Somewhat surprisingly, the better-educated and higher-income respondents are not much more opposed to it than those with less education or income.[15] As Hugo Bedau put it, there is little evidence in the polls that the death penalty is more favored by the "hard hats" than by the professional classes.[16]

Given the fact that blacks are disproportionately the victims of murder, one might suppose that they would favor the death penalty. But quite the opposite is the case. Hans Zeisel reports survey data indicating that only one-third of black men, but over one-half of white men, favor capital punishment. Black women are even less inclined to support the death penalty.[17]

People often adapt their views to support whatever state of affairs happens to exist, and attitudes toward the death penalty may be no exception. Until the Supreme Court decision, California had the death penalty, and almost two-thirds of those polled in that state said they favored its retention. Minnesota has not had the death penalty since the early part of this century, and two-thirds of those polled in that state said they opposed restoring it.

These changes in attitude have been accompanied, over the years, by a trend to greater respect for human life and a tendency to regard execution as somehow barbaric, even if necessary. A hundred years ago a large crowd would turn out for a public hanging; today public opinion barely supports executions at all, and a large majority would probably condemn their being a public spectacle. One hundred fifty years ago, a large number of offenses were punishable by death; today scarcely anyone regards it as remarkable that in general only murder is considered a sufficiently grave crime to warrant the thought of capital punishment. One of the striking facts about the 1972 Supreme

Court decision is that, although only a bare five-man majority found the death penalty as administered to be unconstitutional, eight of the nine Justices indicated their personal opposition to it.

The main issue remains that of justice—the point is not whether capital punishment prevents future crimes, but whether it is a proper and fitting penalty for crimes that have occurred. That is probably as it should be, for such a question forces us to weigh the value we attach to human life against the horror in which we hold a heinous crime. Both that value and that horror change over time. In our modern culture we seem to be uncomfortable about considering these matters, and thus both proponents and opponents of execution fall back on "scientific" assertions about deterrence that are not only dubious but are likely to remain so. The quality of public debate would be substantially improved if all sides recognized this.

Chapter 10

Some Concluding Thoughts

THOSE who have read this far in hopes of finding, not merely a way of thinking about crime, but ways of ending it, have clearly been disappointed. I believe that our society has not done as well as it could have in controlling crime because of erroneous but persistent views about the nature of man and the capacities of his institutions. But I do not believe that, were we to have taken a correct view and as a consequence adopted the most feasible policies, crime would have been eliminated, or even dramatically reduced. Those who argue that we can eliminate crime if only we have the "will" to do so, whether by ending poverty (as the Left argues) or by putting more police on the street and more gallows in our jails (as the Right believes), seriously mistake what we are capable of under even the best of circumstances, and place the blame for our failings precisely where it should not be—on our will power, and by implication on our governing morality.

I argue for a sober view of man and his institutions that

would permit reasonable things to be accomplished, foolish things abandoned, and utopian things forgotten. A sober view of man requires a modest definition of progress. A 20 per cent reduction in robbery would still leave us with the highest robbery rate of almost any Western nation but would prevent about sixty thousand robberies. A small gain for society, a large one for the would-be victims. Yet a 20 per cent reduction is unlikely if we concentrate our efforts on dealing with the causes of crime or even if we concentrate on improving police efficiency. Were we to devote those resources to a strategy that is well within our abilities—namely, to incapacitating a larger fraction of the convicted serious robbers—then not only is a 20 per cent reduction possible, but even larger ones are conceivable.

Most serious crime is committed by repeaters. What we do with first offenders is probably far less important than what we do with habitual offenders. A genuine first offender (and not merely a habitual offender caught for the first time) is in all likelihood a young person who, in the majority of cases, will stop stealing when he gets older. This is not to say we should forgive first offenses, for that would be to license the offense and erode the moral judgments that must underlie any society's attitude toward crime. The gravity of the offense must be appropriately impressed on the first offender, but the effort to devise ways of reeducating or uplifting him in order to insure that he does not steal again is likely to be wasted—both because we do not know how to reeducate or uplift and because most young delinquents seem to reeducate themselves no matter what society does.

After tracing the history of nearly ten thousand Philadelphia boys born in 1945, Marvin Wolfgang and his colleagues at the University of Pennsylvania found that over one-third were picked up by the police for something more serious than a traffic offense, but that 46 per cent of these delinquents had no further police contact after their first offense. Though a third started on crime, nearly half seemed to stop spontaneously—a good thing, because the criminal justice system in that city, already sorely taxed, would in all likelihood have collapsed. Out of the ten thousand boys, however, there were six hundred twenty-seven—only 6 per cent—who committed five or more offenses before they were eighteen. Yet these few chronic offenders accounted for *over half* of all the recorded delinquencies and about *two-thirds* of all the violent crimes committed by the entire cohort.[1]

Only a tiny fraction of all serious crimes lead immediately to an arrest, and only a slightly larger fraction are ultimately "cleared" by an arrest, but this does not mean that the police function is meaningless. Because most serious crime is committed by repeaters, most criminals eventually get arrested. The Wolfgang findings and other studies suggest that the chances of a persistent burglar or robber living out his life, or even going a year, with no arrest are quite small. Yet a large proportion of repeat offenders, as the studies cited in Chapter 8 show, suffer little or no loss of freedom. Whether or not one believes that such penalties, if inflicted, would act as a deterrent, it is obvious that they could serve to incapacitate these offenders and thus, for the period of the incapacitation, prevent them from committing additional crimes.

We have a limited (and declining) supply of detention facilities, and many of those that exist are decrepit, unsafe, and overcrowded. But as important as expanding the supply and improving the decency of the facilities is the need to think seriously about how we wish to allocate those spaces that exist. At present, that allocation is hit or miss. A 1966 survey of over fifteen juvenile correctional institutions revealed that about 30 per cent of the inmates were young persons who had been committed for conduct that would not have been judged criminal were it committed by adults. They were runaways, "stubborn children," or chronic truants—problem children, to be sure, but scarcely major threats to society.[2] Using scarce detention space for them when in Los Angeles over 90 per cent of burglars with a major prior record receive no state prison sentence seems, to put it mildly, anomalous.

Shlomo and Reuel Shinnar have estimated the effect on

crime rates in New York State of a judicial policy other than that followed during the last decade or so. Given the present level of police efficiency and making some assumptions about how many crimes each offender commits per year, they conclude that the rate of serious crime would be only *one-third* what it is today if every person convicted of a serious offense were imprisoned for three years. This reduction would be less if it turned out (as seems unlikely) that most serious crime is committed by first-time offenders, and it would be much greater if the proportion of crimes resulting in an arrest and conviction were increased (as also seems unlikely). The reduction, it should be noted, would be solely the result of incapacitation, making no allowance for such additional reductions as might result from enhanced deterrence or rehabilitation.[3]

The Shinnar estimates are based on uncertain data and involve assumptions that can be challenged. But even assuming they are overly optimistic by a factor of two, a sizable reduction in crime would still ensue. In other countries such a policy of greater incapacitation is in fact followed. A robber arrested in England, for example, is more than three times as likely as one arrested in New York to go to prison. That difference in sentencing does not account for all the difference between English and American crime rates, but it may well account for a substantial fraction of it.

That these gains are possible does not mean that society should adopt such a policy. One would first want to know the costs, in additional prison space and judicial resources, of greater use of incapacitation. One would want to debate the propriety and humanity of a mandatory three-year term; perhaps, in order to accommodate differences in the character of criminals and their crimes, one would want to have a range of sentences from, say, one to five years. One would want to know what is likely to happen to the process of charging and pleading if every person arrested for a serious crime faced a mandatory minimum sentence, however mild. These and other difficult and important questions must first be confronted. But the central fact is that *these are reasonable questions* around which facts can be gathered and intelligent arguments mustered. To discuss them requires us to make few optimistic assumptions about the malleability of human nature, the skills of officials who operate complex institutions, or the capacity of society to improve the fundamental aspects of familial and communal life.

Persons who criticize an emphasis on changing the police and courts to cope with crime are fond of saying that such measures cannot work so long as unemployment and poverty exist. We must acknowledge that we have not done very well at inducting young persons, especially but not only blacks, into the work force. Teenage unemployment rates continue to exceed 20 per cent; though the rate of growth in the youthful component of the population has slowed, their unemployment shows little sign of abating. To a degree, anticrime policies may be frustrated by the failure of employment policies, but it would be equally correct to say that so long as the criminal justice system does not impede crime, efforts to reduce unemployment will not work. If legitimate opportunities for work are unavailable, many young persons will turn to crime; but if criminal opportunities are profitable, many young persons will not take those legitimate jobs that exist. The benefits of work and the costs of crime must be increased simultaneously; to increase one but not the other makes sense only if one assumes that young people are irrational.

One rejoinder to this view is the argument that if legitimate jobs are made absolutely more attractive than stealing, stealing will decline even without any increase in penalties for it. That may be true provided there is no practical limit on the amount that can be paid in wages. Since the average "take" from a burglary or mugging is quite small, it would seem easy to make the income from a job exceed the income from crime. But this neglects the advantages of a criminal income: One works at crime at one's convenience, enjoys the esteem of colleagues who think a "straight" job is stupid and skill at stealing is commendable, looks forward to the occasional "big score" that may make further work unnecessary for weeks, and relishes the risk and adventure associated with theft. The money value of all these benefits—that is, what one who is not shocked by crime would want in cash to forego crime—is hard to estimate, but is almost certainly far larger than what either public or private employers could offer to unskilled or semiskilled young workers. The only alternative for society is to so increase the risks of theft that its value is depreciated below what society can afford to pay in legal wages, and then take whatever steps are necessary to insure that those legal wages are available.

Another rejoinder to the "attack poverty" approach to crime is this: The desire to reduce crime is the worst possible reason for reducing poverty. Most poor persons are not criminals; many are either retired or have regular jobs and lead conventional family lives. The elderly, the working poor, and the willing-to-work poor could benefit greatly from economic conditions and government programs that enhance their incomes without there being the slightest reduction in crime—indeed, if the experience of the 1960s is any guide, there might well be, through no fault of most beneficiaries, an increase in crime. Reducing poverty and breaking up the ghettoes are desirable policies in their own right, whatever their effects on crime. It is the duty of government to devise other measures to cope with crime, not only to permit antipoverty programs to succeed without unfair competition from criminal opportunities, but also to insure that such programs do not inadvertently shift the costs of progress, in terms of higher crime rates, onto innocent parties, not the least of whom are the poor themselves.

One cannot press this economic reasoning too far. Some persons will commit crimes whatever the risks; indeed, for some, the greater the risk the greater the thrill, while others—the alcoholic wife beater, for example—are only dimly aware that there are any risks. But more important than the insensitivity of certain criminal activities to changes in risks and benefits is the impropriety of casting the crime problem wholly in terms of a utilitarian calculus. The most serious offenses are crimes not simply because society finds them inconvenient, but because it regards them with moral horror. To steal, to rape, to rob, to assault—these acts are destructive of the very possibility of society and affronts to the humanity of their victims. It is my experience that parents do not instruct their children to be law abiding merely by pointing to the risks of being caught, but by explaining that these acts are wrong whether or not one is caught. I conjecture that those parents who simply warn their offspring about the risks of crime produce a disproportionate number of young persons willing to take those risks.

Even the deterrent capacity of the criminal justice system depends in no small part on its ability to evoke sentiments of shame in the accused. If all it evoked were a sense of being unlucky, crime rates would be even higher. James Fitzjames Stephens makes the point by analogy. To what extent, he asks, would a man be deterred from theft by the knowledge that by committing it he was exposing himself to one chance in fifty of catching a serious but not fatal illness—say, a bad fever? Rather little, we would imagine—indeed, all of us regularly take risks as great or greater than that: when we drive after drinking, when we smoke cigarettes, when we go hunting in the woods. The criminal sanction, Stephens concludes, "operates not only on the fears of criminals, but upon the habitual sentiments of those who are not criminals. [A] great part of the general detestation of crime . . . arises from the fact that the commission of offenses is associated . . . with the solemn and deliberate infliction of punishment wherever crime is proved." [4]

Much is made today of the fact that the criminal justice system "stigmatizes" those caught up in it, and thus unfairly marks such persons and perhaps even furthers their criminal careers by having "labeled" them as criminals. Whether the labeling process operates in this way is as yet unproved, but it would indeed be unfortunate if society treated a convicted offender in such a way that he had no reasonable alternative but to make crime a career. To prevent this, society ought to insure that one can "pay one's debt" without suffering permanent loss of civil rights, the continuing and pointless indignity of parole supervision, and frustration in being unable to find a job. But doing these things is very different from eliminating the "stigma" from crime. To destigmatize crime would be to lift from it the weight of moral judgment and to make crime simply a particular occupation or avocation which society has chosen to reward less (or perhaps more!) than other pursuits. If there is not stigma attached to an activity, then society has no business making it a crime. Indeed, before the invention of the prison in the late eighteenth and early nineteenth centuries, the stigma attached to criminals was the major deterrent to and principal form of protection from criminal activity. The purpose of the criminal justice system is not to expose would-be criminals to a lottery in which they either win or lose, but to expose them in addition and more importantly to the solemn condemnation of the community should they yield to temptation.

Anyone familiar with the police stations, jails, and courts of some of our larger cities is keenly aware that accused persons caught up in the system are exposed to very little that involves either judgment or solemnity. They are instead processed through a bureaucratic maze in which a bargain is offered and a haggle ensues at every turn—over amount of bail, degree of the charged offense, and the nature of the plea. Much of what observers find objectionable about this process could be alleviated by devoting many more resources to it, so that an ample supply of prosecutors, defense attorneys, and judges were available. That we do not devote those additional resources in a country obsessed with the crime problem is one of the more interesting illustrations of the maxim, familiar to all political scientists, that one cannot predict public policy simply from knowing popular attitudes. Whatever the cause, it remains the case that in New York County (Manhattan) there were in 1973, 31,098 felony arrests to be handled by only 125 prosecutors, 119 public defenders, and 59 criminal court judges. The result was predictable: of those arrested, only 4130 pleaded guilty to or were convicted on a felony charge.

One wonders whether the stigma properly associated with crime retains much deterrent or educative value. My strong inclination is to resist explanations for rising crime that are based on the alleged moral breakdown of society, the community, or the family. I resist in part because most of the families and communities I know have not broken down, and in part because, had they broken down, I cannot imagine any collective action we could take consistent with our civil liberties that would restore a moral consensus, and yet the facts are hard to ignore. Take the family: Over one-third of all black children and one in fourteen of all white children live in single-parent families. Over two million children live in single-parent (usually father absent) households, almost *double* the number of ten years ago. In 1950, 18 per cent of black families were female-headed; in 1969 the proportion had risen to 27 per cent; by 1973 it exceeded 35 per cent. The average income for a single-parent family with children under six years of age was, in 1970, only $3100, well below the official "poverty line." [5]

Studies done in the late 1950s and the early 1960s showed that children from broken homes were more likely than others to become delinquent. In New York State, 58 per cent of the variation in pupil achievement in three hundred schools could be predicted by but three variables—broken homes, overcrowded housing, and parental educational level. Family disorganization, writes Urie Bronfenbrenner, has been shown in thousands of studies to be an "omnipresent overriding factor" in behavior disorders and social pathology. And that disorganization is increasing. [6]

These facts may explain some elements of the rising crime rate that cannot be attributed to the increased number of young persons, high teenage unemployment, or changed judicial policies. The age of persons arrested has been declining for more than fifteen years and the median age of convicted defendants (in jurisdictions for which data are available) has been declining for the last six years. [7] Apparently, the age at which persons begin to commit serious crime has been falling. For some

206

young people, thus, whatever forces weaken their resistance to criminal activity have been increasing in magnitude, and these forces may well include the continued disorganization of the family and the continued deterioration of the social structure of inner city communities.

One wants to be objective, if not optimistic. Perhaps single-parent families today are less disorganized or have a different significance than such families in the past. Perhaps the relationship between family structure and social pathology will change. After all, there now seem to be good grounds for believing that, at least on the East Coast, the heroin epidemic of the 1960s has run its course; though there are still thousands of addicts, the rate of formation of new addicts has slowed and the rate of heroin use by older addicts has dropped. Perhaps other aspects of the relationship among family, personality, and crime will change. Perhaps.

No one can say how much of crime results from its increased profitability and how much from its decreased shamefulness. But one or both factors must be at work, for population changes alone simply cannot account for the increases. Crime in our cities has increased far faster than the number of young people, or poor people, or black people, or just plain people who live in those cities. In short, objective conditions alone, whether demographic or economic, cannot account for the crime increases, though they no doubt contributed to it. Subjective forces—ideas, attitudes, values—played a great part, though in ways hard to define and impossible to measure. An assessment of the effect of these changes on crime would provide a partial understanding of changes in the moral structure of our society.

But to understand is not to change. If few of the demographic factors contributing to crime are subject to planned change, virtually none of the subjective ones are. Though intellectually rewarding, from a practical point of view it is a mistake to think about crime in terms of its "causes" and then to search for ways to alleviate those causes. We must think instead of what it is feasible for a government or a community to do, and then try to discover, by experimentation and observation, which of those things will produce, at acceptable costs, desirable changes in the level of criminal victimization.

There are, we now know, certain things we can change in accordance with our intentions, and certain ones we cannot. We cannot alter the number of juveniles who first experiment with minor crimes. We cannot lower the recidivism rate, though within reason we should keep trying. We are not yet certain whether we can increase significantly the police apprehension rate. We may be able to change the teenage unemployment rate, though we have learned by painful trial and error that doing this is much more difficult than once supposed. We can probably reduce the time it takes to bring an arrested person to trial, even though we have as yet made few serious efforts to do so. We can certainly reduce the arbitrary and socially irrational exercise of prosecutorial discretion over whom to charge and whom to release, and we can most definitely stop pretending that judges know, any better than the rest of us, how to provide "individualized justice." We can confine a larger proportion of the serious and repeat offenders and fewer of the common drunks and truant children. We know that confining criminals prevents them from harming society, and we have grounds for suspecting that some would-be criminals can be deterred by the confinement of others.

Above all, we can try to learn more about what works, and in the process abandon our ideological preconceptions about what *ought* to work. Nearly ten years ago I wrote that the billions of dollars the federal government was then preparing to spend on crime control would be wasted, and indeed might even make matters worse if they were merely pumped into the existing criminal justice system.[8] They were, and they have. In the next ten years I hope we can learn to experiment rather than simply spend, to test our theories rather than fund our fears. This is advice, not simply or even primarily to government—for governments are run by men and women who are under irresistible pressures to pretend they know more than they do—but to my colleagues: academics, theoreticians, writers, advisers. We may feel ourselves under pressure to pretend we know things, but we are also under a positive obligation to admit what we do not know and to avoid cant and sloganizing. The government agency, the Law Enforcement Assistance Administration, that has futilely spent those billions was created in consequence of an act passed by Congress on the advice of a presidential commission staffed by academics, myself included.

It is easy and popular to criticize yesterday's empty hopes and mistaken beliefs, especially if they seemed supportive of law enforcement. It is harder, and certainly most unpopular, to criticize today's pieties and pretensions, especially if they are uttered in the name of progress and humanity. But if we were wrong in thinking that more money spent on the police would bring down crime rates, we are equally wrong in supposing that closing our prisons, emptying our jails, and supporting "community-based" programs will do any better. Indeed, there is some evidence that these steps will make matters worse, and we ignore it at our peril.

Since the days of the crime commission we have learned a great deal, more than we are prepared to admit.[9] Perhaps we fear to admit it because of a newfound modesty about the foundations of our knowledge, but perhaps also because the implications of that knowledge suggest an unflattering view of man. Intellectuals, although they often dislike the common person as an individual, do not wish to be caught saying uncomplimentary things about humankind. Nevertheless, some persons will shun crime even if we do nothing to deter them, while others will seek it out even if we do everything to reform them. Wicked people exist. Nothing avails except to set them apart from innocent people. And many people, neither wicked nor innocent, but watchful, dissembling, and calculating of their opportunities, ponder our reaction to wickedness as a cue to what they might profitably do. We have trifled with the wicked, made sport of the innocent, and encouraged the calculators. Justice suffers, and so do we all.

Notes

Chapter 1 Crime Amidst Plenty:
The Paradox of the Sixties

1. Crime rates used in this chapter are taken from Donald J. Mulvihill and Melvin M. Tumin, eds., *Crimes of Violence*, vol. 11 of a staff report to the National Commission on the Causes and Prevention of Violence (Washington, D.C.: U.S. Government Printing Office, 1969), p. 54.

2. Data on drug use from *Quantitative Analysis of the Heroin Addiction Problem*, a report to the Office of Science and Technology, Executive Office of the President (Arlington, Va.: Institute for Defense Analyses, 1972).

3. The official title of the "Moynihan Report" was *The Negro Family: The Case for National Action* (Washington, D.C.: Office of Policy Planning and Research, U.S. Department of Labor, March 1965). The more recent AFDC figures are from the National Center for Social Statistics, U.S. Department of Health, Education, and Welfare (private communication).

4. Employment figures are from U.S. Department of Labor, Bureau of Labor Statistics, "Youth Unemployment and the Minimum Wage," Bulletin No. 1657 (Washington, D.C.: U.S. Government Printing Office, 1970), pp. 1–6. The phrase quoted appears on p. 5.

5. The figures and comments from Professor Ryder are taken with his permission from a memorandum prepared by him for the President's Science Advisory Committee.

6. The data on Washington, D.C., were supplied by Dr. Robert L. Dupont, M.D., then head of the Narcotics Treatment Administration of that city.

7. Marvin E. Wolfgang, Robert M. Figlio, and Thorsten Sellin, *Delinquency in a Birth Cohort* (Chicago: University of Chicago Press, 1972).

8. Arnold Barnett, Daniel J. Kleitman, and Richard C. Larson, "On Urban Homicide," working paper WP-04-74 (Operations Research Center, Massachusetts Institute of Technology, March 1974).

9. Theodore Ferdinand, "Reported Index Crime Increases Between 1950 and 1965 Due to Urbanization and Changes in the Age Structure of the Population Alone," app. 3 to *Crimes of Violence*, ed. Mulvihill and Tumin, pp. 145–152. See also Llad Phillips, Harold L. Votey, Jr., and Darold Maxwell, "Crime, Youth, and the Labor Market,"

Journal of Political Economy, 80 (May–June 1972): 491–504, and compare Roland Chilton and Adele Spielberger, "Is Delinquency Increasing? Age Structure and the Crime Rate," *Social Forces,* 47 (1971): 487–493.

10. Analyses of the epidemic patterns of heroin addiction include Leon Gibson Hunt, *Heroin Epidemics: A Quantitatve Study of Current Empirical Data,* Monograph MS-3 (Washington, D.C.: Drug Abuse Council, 1973); Robert L. Dupont and Mark H. Greene, "The Dynamics of a Heroin Addiction Epidemic," *Science,* 181 (August 1973): 716–722; and Robert L. Dupont, "Profile of a Heroin-Addiction Epidemic," *New England Journal of Medicine,* 285 (August 1971): 320–324. See also the references for Chapter 8.

Chapter 2   Crime and Community

1. Roger Beardwood, "The New Negro Mood," *Fortune,* 78 (January 1968): 146–151. For some contradictory findings, see Peter K. Eisinger, "The Urban Crisis as a Failure of Community," *Urban Affairs,* 9 (June 1974): 437–461, and my rejoinder on pp. 462–465.

2. Commission on Law Enforcement and the Administration of Justice, *Task Force Report: Assessment of Crime* (Washington, D.C.: U.S. Government Printing Office, 1968), pp. 85–89.

3. I treat here of the function of community in regulating public behavior through face-to-face contact, and stress the rational elements of this regulatory process. There are other meanings—and functions—of community. See, for example, Robert Nisbet, *The Quest for Community* (New York: Oxford University Press, 1953).

4. Daniel Elazar, "Are We a Nation of Cities?" in *A Nation of Cities,* ed. Robert A. Goldwin (Chicago: Rand McNally & Co., 1968), pp. 89–97.

5. "Crime in the Nation's Five Largest Cities," an advance report of the Law Enforcement Assistance Administration, U.S. Department of Justice, Washington, D.C. (April 1974).

6. Sar A. Levitan, William Johnston, and Robert Taggart, *Still a Dream: A Study of Black Progress, Problems, and Prospects* (Cambridge: Harvard University Press, in press), chap. 7.

7. Ibid., chap. 9, and Thomas Sowell, *Black Education: Myths and Tragedies* (New York: David McKay Co., Inc., 1972), p. 119.

8. Orde Coombs, "Three Faces of Harlem," *New York Times Magazine,* November 3, 1974, pp. 32 ff.

Chapter 3   Criminologists

1. President's Commission on Law Enforcement and Administration of Justice, *The Challenge of Crime in a Free Society* (Washington, D.C.: U.S. Government Printing Office, 1967), p. 6.

Notes

2. Ramsey Clark, *Crime in America* (New York: Simon and Schuster, 1970), chap. 4.

3. Edwin H. Sutherland and Donald R. Cressey, *Principles of Criminology*, 7th ed. rev. (Philadelphia: J. B. Lippincott Co., 1966); Richard A. Cloward and Lloyd E. Ohlin, *Delinquency and Opportunity* (New York: Free Press, 1960).

4. Private communication from Professor Ohlin.

5. Sutherland and Cressey, *Principles*, p. 59.

6. Ibid., p. 55.

7. Ibid., pp. 95, 241, 265.

8. Ibid., pp. 150–151.

9. Albert K. Cohen, *Delinquent Boys: The Culture of the Gang* (New York: Free Press, 1955), p. 129.

10. Sheldon and Eleanor Glueck, *Unravelling Juvenile Delinquency* (Cambridge: Harvard University Press, 1950), pp. 279–281.

11. Walter B. Miller, "Lower Class Culture as a Generating Milieu of Gang Delinquency," *Journal of Social Issues* 14 (1958): 15–19. Miller, rare among social scientists, has written insightfully about the relationship of science, ideology, and policy with respect to crime. See, for example, his "Ideology and Criminal Justice Policy: Some Current Issues," *Journal of Criminal Law and Criminology* 64 (1973): 141–162.

12. Cohen, *Delinquent Boys*, p. 25.

13. Sutherland and Cressey, *Principles*, p. 684.

14. Ibid., p. 685.

15. Ibid., pp. 692–693. See also William McCord and Joan McCord, *Origins of Crime* (New York: Columbia University Press, 1959), p. vii, and Edwin Powers and Helen L. Witmer, *An Experiment in the Prevention of Delinquency* (New York: Columbia University Press, 1951).

16. McCord and McCord, *Origins of Crime*, p. 179.

17. Ibid., pp. 181–184.

18. Sutherland and Cressey, *Principles*, p. 367.

19. Ibid., p. 369.

20. Ibid., p. 682.

21. See, for example, Leslie T. Wilkins, *Evaluation of Penal Measures* (New York: Random House, 1969), and Robert Martinson, "What Works? Questions and Answers About Prison Reform," *The Public Interest* (Spring 1974): 22–54.

22. Charles R. Tittle and Charles H. Logan, "Sanctions and Deviance: Evidence and Remaining Questions," *Law and Society Review* (Spring 1973): 371–392.

23. Walter C. Reckless, *The Crime Problem*, 4th ed. (New York: Appleton-Century-Crofts, 1967), p. 508.

24. Tittle and Logan, "Sanctions and Deviance," p. 385.

25. Cloward and Ohlin, *Delinquency and Opportunity*, p. 86.

26. Ibid., p. 93.

27. Ibid., p. 211.

28. Ibid., p. 150.

29. Ibid., pp. 152, 154.

30. Lloyd E. Ohlin, "Report on the President's Commission on Law Enforcement and Administration of Justice" (Paper presented to the American Sociological Association, August 1973), p. 26.

31. Ibid., pp. 27, 28.
32. Ibid., p. 29.
33. Robert Martinson, "Letter to the Editor," *Commentary* 58 (October 1974): 12.
34. Ibid., p. 32.

Chapter 4   Politicians

1. A stimulating and factual analysis of the political significance of crime and other aspects of what the authors called the "Social Issue" in the politics of the late 1960s is Richard M. Scammon and Ben J. Wattenberg, *The Real Majority* (New York: Coward-McCann, 1970).

Chapter 5   The Police and Crime

1. See, for example, Albert J. Reiss, Jr., *The Police and the Public* (New Haven: Yale University Press, 1971), p. 71.
2. The report on Operation 25 is from a brochure published by the New York City Police Department.
3. J. A. Bright, *Beat Patrol Experiment*, Report No. 8/69 of the Police Research and Development Branch, Home Office, London, England (July 1969).
4. S. J. Press, *Some Effects of an Increase in Police Manpower in the 20th Precinct of New York City*, Report No. R-704-NYC (New York: Rand Institute, 1971).
5. Jan M. Chaiken, Michael W. Lawless, and Keith A. Stevenson, *The Impact of Police Activity on Crime: Robberies in the New York City Subway System*, Report No. R-1424-NYC (New York: Rand Institute, 1974).
6. The Ennis and Biderman studies were both reports to the President's Commission on Law Enforcement and Administration of Justice. Philip H. Ennis, *Criminal Victimization in the United States: A Report of a National Survey*, and Albert D. Biderman et al., *Report on a Pilot Study in the District of Columbia on Victimization and Attitudes Toward Law Enforcement* (Washington, D.C.: U.S. Government Printing Office, 1967).
7. An overview of efforts at team policing is Lawrence W. Sherman et al., *Team Policing* (Washington, D.C.: The Police Foundation, 1973).
8. Data supplied by the New York Police Department.

Chapter 6   The Police and the Community

1. Gary T. Marx, *Protest and Prejudice* (New York: Harper & Row, 1967), p. 36.
2. Philip H. Ennis, *Criminal Victimization in the United States*, a research study submitted to the President's Commission on Law Enforcement and Administration of Justice (Chicago: National Opinion Research Center, 1967), p. 56.
3. President's Commission on Law Enforcement and Administration of Justice, *Task*

Notes

Force Report: The Police (Washington, D.C.: U.S. Government Printing Office, 1967), p. 146.

4. Albert D. Biderman et al., *Report on a Pilot Study in the District of Columbia on Victimization and Attitudes Toward Law Enforcement*, a research study submitted to the President's Commission on Law Enforcement and Administration of Justice (Washington, D.C.: U.S. Government Printing Office, 1967), p. 145.

5. Albert J. Reiss, Jr., "Public Perceptions and Recollections About Crime, Law Enforcement, and Criminal Justice," in *Studies in Crime and Law Enforcement in Major Metropolitan Areas*, a research study submitted to the President's Commission on Law Enforcement and Administration of Justice (Ann Arbor: University of Michigan Survey Research Center, 1967), vol. 1, sec. 2, p. 55.

6. Angus Campbell and Howard Schuman, "Racial Attitudes in Fifteen American Cities," in *Supplemental Studies for the National Advisory Commission on Civil Disorders* (Washington, D.C.: U.S. Government Printing Office, 1968), pp. 41–45.

7. President's Commission, *Task Force Report: The Police*, p. 147.

8. Campbell and Schuman, "Racial Attitudes," p. 44.

9. Ibid.

10. President's Commission, *Task Force Report: The Police*, p. 148.

11. *Fortune*, January 1968, p. 148.

12. *New York Times*, December 13, 1968.

13. *Detroit News*, February 25, 1969.

14. Ennis, *Criminal Victimization*, pp. 55–56.

15. James Q. Wilson, "Police Morale, Reform, and Citizen Respect: The Chicago Case," in *The Police*, ed. David J. Bordua (New York: John Wiley & Sons, 1967), p. 17. See also Jerome H. Skolnick, *Justice Without Trial* (New York: John Wiley & Sons, 1966), pp. 9–65.

16. Peter H. Rossi et al., "Between White and Black: The Faces of American Institutions in the Ghetto," in *Supplemental Studies*, p. 104.

17. Ibid., p. 106. See also David H. Bayley and Harold Mendelsohn, *Minorities and the Police* (New York: Free Press, 1969), pp. 45–46.

18. Rossi, "Between White and Black," p. 106.

19. Ibid., pp. 109, 111.

20. Donald J. Black and Albert J. Reiss, Jr., "Police Control of Juveniles," *American Sociological Review* 35 (February 1970): 63–77.

21. Frank F. Furstenberg, Jr., and Charles F. Wellford, "Calling the Police: The Evaluation of Police Service," *Law and Society Review* 7 (Spring 1973): 402.

22. Paul E. Smith and Richard O. Hawkins, "Victimization, Types of Citizen-Police Contacts, and Attitudes Toward the Police," *Law and Society Review* 8 (Fall 1973): 140.

23. Ibid., p. 142.

24. Furstenberg and Wellford, "Calling the Police," p. 402.

25. Richard O. Hawkins, "Who Called the Cops?: Decisions to Report Criminal Victimization," *Law and Society Review* 7 (Spring 1973): 441, and Richard L. Block, "Police Action, Support for the Police, and Support for Civil Liberties" (Paper delivered at the annual meeting of the American Sociological Association, September 1970).

26. Reiss, "Police Perceptions," pp. 20, 39, 47, 55, 75.

27. Albert J. Reiss, Jr., *The Police and the Public* (New Haven: Yale University Press, 1971), p. 77.

28. Arthur Niederhofer, *Behind the Shield* (Garden City, N.Y.: Doubleday & Company, 1967), p. 235.

29. Herbert A. Shepard, "Changing Interpersonal and Intergroup Relations in Organizations," in *Handbook of Organizations*, ed. James G. March (Chicago: Rand McNally & Co., 1965), pp. 1132–1141.

30. Harold J. Leavitt, "Applied Organizational Change in Industry," in March, *Handbook of Organizations*, p. 1167, and Morton A. Lieberman et al., *Encounter Groups: First Facts* (New York: Basic Books, 1973), chap. 16.

31. Charles Sklarsky, "The Police-Community Relations Program" (Senior honor's thesis, Department of Government, Harvard University, March 1968).

32. David Wellman, "Putting on the Poverty Program," Radical Education Project, Ann Arbor, Mich., n.d.

33. Reiss, *The Police and the Public*, pp. 207–212, and James Q. Wilson, *Varieties of Police Behavior* (Cambridge: Harvard University Press, 1968), pp. 288–290.

34. Bernard Cohen and Jan M. Chaiken, *Police Background Characteristics and Performance*, Report No. R-999-DOJ (New York: Rand Institute, 1972). See also Melany E. Baehr et al., *Psychological Assessment of Patrolman Qualifications in Relation to Field Performance*, a report to the Office of Law Enforcement Assistance of the U.S. Department of Justice from the Industrial Relations Center of the University of Chicago, mimeographed, 1968.

35. I have been impressed, for example, with the work of the Applied Psychology Workshop of the Police Academy of the Chicago Police Department, although I am not aware of any systematic evaluation of its effects. To my regret, but not to my surprise, it appears to have been terminated.

36. David J. Bordua and Larry L. Tifft, "Citizen Interviews, Organizational Feedback and Police Community Relations Decisions," *Law and Society Review* 6 (November 1971): esp. 162–168.

37. Donald J. Black and Albert J. Reiss, Jr., "Patterns of Behavior in Police and Citizen Transactions," in *Studies of Crime and Law Enforcement in Major Metropolitan Areas*, a research study submitted to the President's Commission on Law Enforcement and Administration of Justice (Ann Arbor: University of Michigan Survey Research Center, 1967), vol. 2, p. 87.

Chapter 7   Heroin

1. Student task force reports prepared at Harvard University, American University, the University of Southern California, the University of Pennsylvania, Southern Methodist University, Washington University, and the University of California at Berkeley are on file at the Sloan Foundation, New York City.

2. Thomas H. Bewley et al., "Mortality and Morbidity from Heroin Dependence," *British Medical Journal* 1 (March 23, 1968): 725–732.

3. Isador Chein et al., *The Road to H.* (New York: Basic Books, 1964).

4. Patrick H. Hughes and Gail A. Crawford, "A Contagious Disease Model for

Notes

Researching and Intervening in Heroin Epidemics," *Archives of General Psychiatry* 27 (August 1972): 149–155, and Patrick Hughes et al., "The Natural History of a Heroin Epidemic," *American Journal of Public Health* 62 (July 1972): 995–1001. See also Leon Gibson Hunt, *Recent Spread of Heroin Use in the United States*, Monograph MS–10 (Washington, D.C.: Drug Abuse Council, 1974).

5. Lee Robbins and G. Murphy, "Drug Use in a Normal Population of Young Negro Men," *American Journal of Public Health* 57, (September 1967): 1580–1596.

6. E. Preble and J. Casey, "Taking Care of Business—The Heroin User's Life on the Street," *International Journal of the Addictions* 4 (March 1969): 1–24.

7. John A. O'Donnell, "Narcotic Addiction and Crime," *Social Problems* 13 (Spring 1966): 374–385.

8. Max Singer and S. Newitt, *Policy Concerning Drug Abuse in New York State*, 3 vols. (New York: Hudson Institute, 1970).

9. Max Singer, "The Vitality of Mythical Numbers," *The Public Interest* (Spring 1971): 3–9.

10. George Vaillant, "A Twelve Year Follow-Up of New York Narcotic Addicts: I. The Relation of Treatment to Outcome," *American Journal of Psychiatry* 122 (1966): 727–737.

11. Griffith Edwards, "The British Approach to the Treatment of Heroin Addiction," *Lancet* 1 (1969): 768–772.

12. Edgar May, "Drugs Without Crime," *Harpers* (July 1971): 60–65.

13. I. David Wheat, Jr., "Heroin Abuse in Boston," in *Heroin Abuse in Boston*, a report of a Harvard University task force (Public Policy Program, Kennedy School of Government, Harvard, 1972).

14. Hughes and Crawford, "A Contagious Disease Model"; Hughes et al., "The Natural History."

15. Robert Schasre, "Cessation Patterns Among Neophyte Heroin Users," *International Journal of the Addictions* 1 (1966): 23–33.

16. Hughes, "A Contagious Disease Model." See also Patrick H. Hughes et al., "The Medical Management of a Heroin Epidemic," *Archives of General Psychiatry* 27 (November 1972): 585–591.

17. Frances R. Gearing, "Successes and Failures in Methadone Maintenance Treatment of Heroin Addiction in New York City," *Proceedings*, Third National Conference on Methadone Treatment (NIMH), Public Health Service Publication No. 2172 (1970).

18. James Vorenberg and Irving F. Lukoff, "Addiction, Crime, and the Criminal Justice System," *Federal Probation* 37 (December 1973): 3–7. See also Gila J. Hayim, Irving Lukoff, and Debra Quatrone, *Heroin Use and Crime in a Methadone Maintenance Program* (Washington, D.C.: U.S. Department of Justice, Law Enforcement Assistance Administration, February 1973).

19. Edwards, "The British Approach."

20. Bewley, "Mortality and Morbidity." See also the recent follow-up study of addicts in British clinics, G. V. Stimson, *Heroin and Behavior* (New York: John Wiley & Sons, 1973).

21. Lee N. Robbins, "A Follow-Up of Vietnam Drug Users," Interim Final Report on Contract HSM–42–72–75 (Washington, D.C.: Special Action Office for Drug Abuse Prevention, 1973).

Chapter 8   Courts and Corrections

1. Jacob Belkin, Alfred Blumstein, and William Glass, "Recidivism as a Feedback Process: An Analytical Model and Empirical Validation," *Journal of Criminal Justice* 1 (1973): 7–26.

2. Marvin E. Wolfgang, Robert M. Figlio, and Thorsten Sellin, *Delinquency in a Birth Cohort* (Chicago: University of Chicago Press, 1972).

3. Jan M. Chaiken, Michael W. Lawless, and Keith A. Stevenson, *The Impact of Police Activity on Crime: Robberies on the New York City Subway System*, Report No. R–1424–NYC (New York: Rand Institute, 1974), p. 65.

4. Harold D. Lasswell and Jeremiah B. McKenna, *The Impact of Organized Crime on an Inner City Community* (New York: The Policy Sciences Center, 1972), p. 203.

5. Donald J. Newman, "Pleading Guilty for Considerations: A Study of Bargain Justice," *Journal of Criminal Law, Criminology, and Police Science* 46 (1956): 780ff.

6. Martin A. Levin, "Urban Politics and Policy Outcomes: The Criminal Courts," in *Criminal Justice*, ed. George F. Cole (No. Scituate, Mass.: Duxbury Press, 1972), p. 335.

7. Dean V. Babst and John W. Mannering, "Probation Versus Imprisonment for Similar Types of Offenders," *Journal of Research in Crime and Delinquency* 2 (July 1965): 61ff.

8. Peter W. Greenwood et al., *Prosecution of Adult Felony Defendants in Los Angeles County: A Policy Perspective*, Report No. R–1127–DOJ (Santa Monica: Rand, 1973), p. 109.

9. Lasswell and McKenna, *Impact of Organized Crime*, p. 185.

10. I. David Wheat, Jr., "Heroin Abuse in Boston," in *Heroin Abuse in Boston*, a report of a Harvard University task force (Public Policy Program, Kennedy School of Government, Harvard, 1972).

11. Martin A. Levin, "Crime, Punishment, and Social Science," *The Public Interest* (Spring 1972): 96–103.

12. Ronald H. Beattie and Charles K. Bridges, "Superior Court Probation and/or Jail Sample," Bureau of Criminal Statistics, State of California (Sacramento, 1970).

13. Levin, "Crime, Punishment, and Social Science."

14. *New York Times*, September 26, 1972, p. 1.

15. President's Commission on Law Enforcement and Administration of Justice, *The Challenge of Crime in a Free Society* (Washington, D.C.: U.S. Government Printing Office, 1967), pp. vii, 170.

16. James Robinson and Gerald Smith, "The Effectiveness of Correctional Programs," *Crime and Delinquency* (January 1971): 67–80.

17. Robert Martinson, "What Works?—Questions and Answers About Prison Reform," *The Public Interest* (Spring 1974): 22–54.

18. R. G. Hood, "Research on the Effectiveness of Punishments and Treatments," in *Crime and Justice*, ed. Leon Radzinowicz and Marvin E. Wolfgang (New York: Basic Books, 1971), vol. 3, pp. 159–182.

19. Walter C. Bailey, "Correctional Outcome: An Evaluation of 100 Reports," in *Crime and Justice*, ed. Radzinowicz and Wolfgang, vol. 3, p. 190.

218

Notes

20. Leslie T. Wilkins, *Evaluation of Penal Measures* (New York: Random House, 1969), p. 78.

21. Citizens' Inquiry on Parole and Criminal Justice, *Report on New York Parole* (New York City, March 1974). See also Robert W. Kastenmeier and Howard C. Eglit, "Parole Release Decision-Making," *American University Law Review* 22 (Spring 1973): 477–525.

22. *Statistical Abstract of the United States, 1972* (Washington, D.C.: U.S. Government Printing Office, 1972), p. 161.

23. While the crime rate in New York was rising, the state prison population declined between 1960 and 1970 by 30 per cent.

24. Greenwood, et al., *Prosecution of Adult Felony Defendants*, p. 110.

25. George E. Antunes and E. Lee Hunt, "The Impact of Certainty and Severity of Punishment on Levels of Crime in American States: An Extended Analysis" (Paper presented to the annual meeting of the American Political Science Association, September 1972). Other reviews of this and even more recent literature include Gordon Tullock, "The Deterrence of Crime," *The Public Interest* (Summer 1974): 103–111, and Charles R. Tittle and Charles H. Logan, "Sanctions and Deviance: Evidence and Remaining Questions," *Law and Society Review* 7 (Spring 1973): 371–392. The entire subject of deterrence is thoughtfully considered by Franklin E. Zimring and Gordon J. Hawkins, *Deterrence* (Chicago: University of Chicago Press, 1973).

26. Isaac Ehrlich, "The Deterrent Effect of Criminal Law Enforcement," *Journal of Legal Studies* 1 (1972): 259–276.

27. On drinking and traffic laws, see Johannes Andeneas, "The General Preventive Effects of Punishment," *University of Pennsylvania Law Review* 114 (May 1966): 949–983, and studies cited therein.

28. Belton Fleisher, *The Economics of Delinquency* (Chicago: Quadrangle Books, 1966), and Llad Phillips, Harold L. Votey, Jr., and Darold Maxwell, "Crime, Youth and the Labor Market: An Econometric Study," *Journal of Political Economy*, 80 (May–June 1972): 491–504.

29. Ehrlich, "The Deterrent Effect of Criminal Law Enforcement."

30. James Fitzjames Stephens, *A History of the Criminal Law of England* (New York: Burt Franklin, 1973), vol. 2, p. 79 (first published in 1883).

Chapter 9 The Death Penalty

1. *Furman* v. *Georgia*, 408 U.S. 238 (1972).

2. Ernest van den Haag, "On Deterrence and the Death Penalty," *Ethics* 78 (July 1968): 280–288.

3. Hugo Adam Bedau, "The Death Penalty as a Deterrent: Argument and Evidence," *Ethics* 80 (April 1970): 205–217.

4. Hugo Adam Bedau, *The Death Penalty in America* (Garden City, N.Y.: Doubleday, 1967), pp. 434–452.

5. Hugo Adam Bedau, "The Death Penalty in America," *Federal Probation* 35 (June 1971): 32–43.

6. Marvin E. Wolfgang, Arlene Kelly, and Hans C. Nolde, "Comparison of the Executed and Commuted Among Admissions to Death Row," *Journal of Criminal Law, Criminology, and Police Science* 53 (1962): 301–311.

7. Marvin E. Wolfgang and Marc Riedel, "Race, Judicial Discretion, and the Death Penalty," *Annals of the American Academy of Political and Social Science* 407 (May 1973): 119–133.

8. Thorsten Sellin, *Capital Punishment* (New York: Harper & Row, 1967), esp. pp. 135–160.

9. Robert H. Dann, "The Deterrent Effect of Capital Punishment," Bulletin 29, Friends Social Service Series (Philadelphia, 1935); Leonard D. Savitz, "A Study in Capital Punishment," *Journal of Criminal Law, Criminology, and Police Science* 49 (1959): 338–341; William E. Graves, "A Doctor Looks at Capital Punishment," in *The Death Penalty in America*, ed. Hugo Adam Bedau (Chicago: Aldine, 1964), pp. 322–332.

10. Donald R. Campion, "Does the Death Penalty Protect State Police?" in Bedau, *Death Penalty in America*, pp. 301–315.

11. Department of Justice, Bureau of Prisons, *National Prisoner Statistics*, Bulletin No. 46: "Capital Punishment, 1930–1970," in *Sourcebook of Criminal Justice Statistics* (Washington, D.C.: U.S. Government Printing Office, 1973), p. 462.

12. Quoted in Franklin E. Zimring and Gordon J. Hawkins, *Deterrence* (Chicago: University of Chicago Press, 1973), pp. 30–32.

13. Los Angeles Police Department, "A Study on Capital Punishment" (February 1971).

14. Franklin E. Zimring, "The Medium Is the Message," *Journal of Legal Studies* 1 (1972): 97–123.

15. Hazel Erskine, "The Polls: Capital Punishment," *Public Opinion Quarterly* 34 (Summer 1970): 290–307.

16. Bedau, "The Death Penalty in America," *Federal Probation*, p. 35.

17. Zeisel is quoted in Erskine, "The Polls," pp. 296–297.

Chapter 10 Some Concluding Thoughts

1. Marvin E. Wolfgang, "Crime in a Birth Cohort," in *The Aldine Crime and Justice Annual, 1973*, ed. Sheldon L. Messinger (Chicago: Aldine, 1973), pp. 110–112.

2. Shlomo and Reuel Shinnar, "A Simplified Model for Estimating the Effects of the Criminal Justice System on the Control of Crime," School of Engineering, The City College of New York, 1974. Unpublished.

3. William H. Sheridan, "Juveniles Who Commit Non-Criminal Acts," *Federal Probation* 31 (1967): 26–30, and Edwin M. Lemert, *Instead of Court* (Rockville, Md.: Center for Studies in Crime and Delinquency, National Institute of Mental Health, 1971), pp. 13–14.

4. James Fitzjames Stephens, A *History of the Criminal Law of England* (New York: Burt Franklin, 1973), vol. 2, pp. 80–81 (first published in 1883).

5. Urie Bronfenbrenner, "The Origins of Alienation," *Scientific American* 231

Notes

(August 1974): 53. See also Thomas P. Monahan, "Family Status and the Delinquent Child," *Social Forces* 35 (1957): 250–258.

6. Bronfenbrenner, "Origins of Alienation," p. 56.

7. Charles F. Wellford, "Age Composition and the Increase in Recorded Crime," *Criminology* 11 (1973): 61–70, and Benjamin Avi-Itzhak and Reuel Shinnar, "Quantitative Models in Crime Control," *Journal of Criminal Justice* 1 (1973): 196–197.

8. James Q. Wilson, "Crime and Law Enforcement," in *Agenda for the Nation*, ed. Kermit Gordon (Washington, D.C.: Brookings Institution, 1968), pp. 198–201.

9. Note, for example, the remarks of Deputy Attorney General Laurence Silberman urging that all LEAA projects be subject to careful evaluation (*LEAA Newsletter*, August–September 1974).

Index

223

Index

Index

227

Index

229

Index